Desert
Experience

A SPIRITUAL MEMOIR

William E. McNamara

Desert Experience: A Spiritual Memoir
Copyright © 2023 William E. McNamara

Visit our website at
www.StillwaterPress.com
for more information.

ISBN: 978-1-960505-45-3
Library of Congress Control Number: 2023910725
1 2 3 4 5 6 7 8 9 10
Written by William E. McNamara.
Cover design by Matthew St. Jean.
Published by Stillwater River Publications,
Pawtucket, RI, USA.

Names: McNamara, William, author.
Title: Desert experience: a spiritual memoir / William E. McNamara
Identifiers: ISBN: 978-1-960505-45-3 (paperback) | LCCN: 20239104725
Subjects: LCSH: McNamara, William—Religion | Priests—Biography. | Prayer | Contemplation | Spirituality | Theology | Enlightenment | Experience (Religion) | LCGFT:
Autobiographies. | Self-help publications.
Classification: LCC: BX4705.M476544-A3 2023 | DDC: 282.092—dc23

To Rebecca, Maria and Ramon,
Father Simon, Theresia, Dr. Gary, Leslie, Bonny,
and all who took great care of William in his final years.

Contents

Contents

Acknowledgements

Particular thanks to Tom G., Ray and Marion, and Tom C. Thanks to all who transcribed and typed William's handwritten manuscript chapters. Special thanks to editor Trisha Giramma for bringing this book to print.

Introduction

The Last Contemplative

Snow falls unexpectedly in the Lamoille Valley. It is a gentle event, with flakes large enough to be seen across the yard against a backdrop of pines and mountains. The snow is widely spaced with a nearly vertical descent, sufficiently slow to allow the ticking mantle clock to mark several well-spaced seconds as tufts of white trace a journey across the window's view. A fluffed out pair of mourning doves perch in a tree near the window, undisturbed by the snow.

These days abide in a holy time of year, where events of two millennia previous conjoined God and Humanity in family. Labored breath gave way to baby's coo in a *stille nochte*. And life on Earth has never been the same.

In our own time, monumental challenges, from a global pandemic to extreme storms, tides, and fires due to climate change, have rocked our status quo. Other changes have taken place as well, as any evening news program will confirm. But quietly, beyond the news coverage, monasteries—centers of contemplative prayer—are closing one after another. The reasons are mostly due to a change in our culture resulting in a decline in young people willing to dedicate themselves to a life of prayer, and the death of elderly religious who have given it their all. So, in this twenty-first century there are few living examples and fewer mentors.

Who then, will be the Last Contemplative? And why might anyone care?

Because when contemplatives behold the Real in a long, loving look, ego thins and is displaced by the Holy One. This is no eerie soothsaying, no smoke and mirrors, but a grounded earthiness full of common sense. Contemplatives steer toward that which is whole and without contradiction; they find the sacred in muck and mire as well as in the fragile texture of life.

Jesus himself thought solitary prayer was so important that he suspended his healing and preaching ministries for time alone. These periods of prayer allowed Jesus to prepare for, and indeed make possible, the major events described in the Gospels.

In this way, it makes all the sense in the world that a contemplative life is the only meaningful framework for a life of action. Whether the action is continual intercessory prayer or physical intervention in the world, contemplative prayer is the means to abandon selfish interests and dispose oneself before the Divine. This personal experience of God is what McNamara uses to define a mystic, a soul whose gaze is not limited by the ego but, at least momentarily, is defenseless before the onslaught of a loving God.

And so, the loss of contemplatives and special sacred places is of grave concern. How can we, who live in a digital age of hyperstimulation, learn to slow down, to become still before the Living God? How can anyone—from the City or Wilderness, or in any stage of life—embark on this journey? How can one step into action without wreaking havoc?

In his final year, McNamara saw his ultimate challenge as answering these questions in a way that others could understand. Despite illness and a body wracked in pain, he combed through all his earlier writings and new additions, selecting those which could become not an instruction manual, but a guide. He wished to show that contemplative prayer was accessible and worthwhile. McNamara titled the book *Desert Experience* because he wanted to illuminate those conditions in life that could lead one to contemplative prayer, just as physical deserts with their rigors and risks had provided early holy men and women with an environment to focus on life and prayer.

McNamara had hoped to see laity step into roles and paths previously restricted to clergy and professed religious. Because, for the divine-human adventure to continue, there can be no Last Contemplative. Indeed, it is a vocation to which we each are called.

S.C. Adamowicz, Ph.D.
Lamoille Valley, Vermont
December 2022

Desert Experience

Chapter One

Do We Need Religion?

*I*n terms of conveniences, commodities, commerce and comfort, we as a nation, or even a Western civilization, have progressed immensely. G.K. Chesterton warns us, however, that "progress is the mother of all problems," the largest being the dumbing down of society, its ever growing pathology, and its feverish, mindless activity. Action without contemplation is blind. That leaves us with moralism. We are a correct and legal people with no high morals—no intimacy, ecstasy, or fecundity. We are so driven; we are unable to live deliberately.

Holiness comes from deep relatedness. Such profound I-Thou relationships grow only in stillness and decline in busy-ness[1]. In a hurried, unexamined life, we

---

[1] *I-Thou* is the title of a book by Martin Buber, published in English in 1937. It is a core work for philosophy and theology, discussing the nature of relationships—whether between

1

suffer dehumanization. We need to rediscover our distinctive noble human nature, ripe for divinization, which happens when we are deeply related to one another and to the One who sustains us by his love—a love that not only refreshes but also remakes us, however painfully.

Our relatedness is so shallow, narrow and utilitarian; even spousal lovers use one another—a sophisticated form of squalor. Our plight is to live in an alienated age, alienated from our inner selves. Consequently—although communication proliferates—communion, the fundamental human act, is in peril. Over-communication precludes the apotheosis—even the rudiments—of communion. Without divine-human intimacy, is life meaningful?

We need to create an environment—an Erosphere[2]—in the Wilderness, where becoming exquis-

---

two people or with the earth or sky or creature (e.g. a tree). I-Thou relationships are sacred, with the ultimate being an I-Thou relationship with God. (Wikipedia.org accessed December 13, 2017).

[2] Eros is defined later in this chapter. For some readers, the notion of "eros" or "Eros" may lead to discomfort, probably due to the common, modern association with erotica. As the reader will find, this is not what McNamara had in mind. Indeed, so taken was McNamara by the concept of eros that he had planned to write an entire book on the subject. But time grew short and so he began to focus on the current summary of his insights into the Christo-Human adventure. References

itely human is an imminent possibility. Humanness involves the keen awareness of the relatedness of all creatures: all have rights and deserve from humans a reverent response.

The Trinity is the model and source of this interdependent life among "interviduals" (to us a barbarous neologism). Christ came to make us conscious of the vitality of the Spirit. "God became human so we could become God." What did the Fathers and Doctors of the Church and the great Oriental mystics mean by that stunning statement? Simply this: We are not like God autonomously, but in God ontologically. Human growth is becoming Godlike. Jesus did not come looking for fans. He inserted his spirit into the World dynamism for the eternal emergence of Christ-men and Christ-women.

An Oriental mystic would say, "This is Tao." Or as any good guy on the street would say, "This is it, man." *Tat tuam isi.* Mark Twain said, "There was only one Christian and He died a long time ago." Well, yes.

---

to "eros" in this chapter are but a glimpse into the larger work he had planned. The primary puzzle that may have instigated his interest in "eros" was the Incarnation itself. If flesh did not matter, if the whole business was about Spirit, then why the Incarnation? Why the fleshiness of humanity, dogs, cats, indeed the planet and cosmos? The answer is that flesh, stuffness, the suchness of being, does matter. And as that whole kit and caboodle is drawn to God, therein lies eros. Maybe. If I have it right. But read on and set your own biases and baggage aside in order to see the *care* that is described herein.

But J. D. Salinger unpacked that poetic, pungent insight in a stringent, straight statement: "See Christ and you are a Christian; all else is talk." To see him is to love him, to love him is to be shaped by his spirit. Such living experience transforms each one of us into the contemporary Christ, worshipfully aware of the Ineffable.

This is the contemplative life: a long, loving look at the real; a personal, passionate participation in the vivifying cosmotheandric Presence; the Creative Act at the heart of the universe, uniting everything. From this source alone comes saving action—love-making and justice-making.

In the fourth century, thousands of lay people went into the Wilderness—untamed, unspoiled places in the mountains and deserts—not to save their souls, but to become human, live freely, and relate to wild things; including, and especially, God. In a word, to pray. They did not go for comfort (praying is not pretty poetics). Rather, for a howling penitence, a daring adventure, a joyful exploration into the ultimate—the swirling sheerness of being into boundless love. More than anything else today, we need this desert experience, not to pump life back into religion, but to rethink and reform the military-industrial complex, the socio-political arena, our obsessive-compulsive disorder, and the meretricious utilitarian aspects of schooling.

All our merely human efforts based on technological progress and political puissance have failed. A paradigmatic shift, even a radical mutation, is necessary. Metanoia or catastrophe, sanctity or suicide. The choice is simple. The result is holiness or horridness.

The fundamental form of human disability is selfishness. So far, human ingenuity has discovered only one way of curing this basic disease. Our very existence needs to be shaken at the core by a God-given state of "being beside oneself." The Christian conception of human, the psychoanalytical knowledge of human nature, and the mystical insights of the Great Traditions—Biblical, Plato-Socratic, Oriental, and Western—leave us with one unwavering conviction: the demon rampant in the world today can be overcome by prayer and penance.

And that happened to be the first message of Jesus. Today more than ever this teaching is practical, relevant, and salvific. It should be our primary concern, our trenchant practice. Life is becoming less and less important precisely because the search for meaning—this hunger for substance and mystical[3], personal experience

---

[3] Mysticism and in turn, the mystic, was central to McNamara's life and work. See for example the section on Mystical Experience in *The Human Adventure* (1976 Image Books, pg 132), where he states, "The mark of a mystic is to *be held and captivated* by a personal, intimate and experiential union with God, not just to *know about it*." On numerous other occasions, McNamara has referred to the mystical experience as an awareness of the "personal, passionate presence of God." Also in *The Human Adventure*, McNamara describes the *earthy mystic* as an ordinary or even worldly person. His greatest earthy mystics were Mary and Joseph, "who

of God—is not all-important. If God is not supremely, attractively there, then we are nowhere.

The deepest and most dire human cry—as philosopher-theologian Joseph Pieper pinpoints in his luminous book, *Divine Madness*—is for a plangent, robust resistance to the attempt to establish the autocratic Rule of Man. For Man deludes himself that he possesses sovereign powers over the world and himself, thus squandering his real existential patrimony, which is achieved and preserved only through a willingly accepted openness for divine revelation—for the salutary pain of catharsis, for the recollecting power of the fine arts, for the emotional shock brought about by *eros* and *caritas*. In short, through the attitude rooted in the mysterious experience that Plato called *theia mania*, or "God-intoxicated."

To be merely theoretical at this point would be almost useless. So let me offer you a concrete experiential example: The Spiritual Life Instance[4] is a research center for the study and practice of mystical life (Julian Center), and a unique contemplative retreat house for lay hermits (Corpus Christi).

Hence, there are no fustian, no rigid or busy programs. Just a place to do nothing, to be. A place of

---

became saints by taking good care of Jesus. They had no mystical techniques. Their lives were unpretentious, almost unnoticeable" (pg. 151).

[4] The Spiritual Life Instance was founded by William McNamara in 2004 and was dedicated to pursuing and celebrating the Divine aspects of the human adventure.

learning (in-depth theology) and leisure (mystical life). Once a year, here at Corpus Christi Hermitage in Borrego Springs, California, experts on life will come to share significant insights based on research and experience[5]. Results will be published. Otherwise, the silent, solitary focus is on beauty, with its promise of eternal beatitude.

The core community—mostly lay people—will live together in solitude, loosely organized, but united by the Spiritual Life Instance's simple rule: specific reading, daily prayer, and a contagious love. Plus—and this is critical—leisurely, voluntary work and self-oblivious play.

Such contemplative life in the secular world injects the sacred into the profane, divinizes the human, and hallows the technological, industrial, political world. It will be delightfully informal but more educative than schoolish endeavors and more religious than religion.

The crucial challenge will be fidelity—to God, to the Mystical Body of Christ, to revelation transmitted by the great religious traditions, as well as the brand new prompting of the Holy Spirit. But above all, to one another (which involves God)—and unflagging, unconditional loyalty. Communities rise or fall depending on their trust in and fidelity to one another.

---

[5] Corpus Christi Hermitage was closed following Abba Willie's death in 2015.

A single instance of perfidy will threaten the existence of the community.

Openness, bigness, and God-centeredness will preclude the pettiness, cowardice, and banality that shrink the moral grandeur and shred the spiritual audacity of a discipleship designed by the Deity Itself for the sake of the Kingdom: an Erosphere—an enlightened openness to the inflowing of the Spirit on the searching soul of human beings.

It is up to us to replace the Empire (comprised of mediocrity, manipulation, and mendacity) with the Kingdom—the resurrected order of being where Love dictates everything. I certainly don't mean a loopy love, but enlightened love. T.S. Eliot was right: The price for enlightenment is not less than everything. In that case there's no hope for cowards. So the cardinal virtues of SLI at Corpus Christi Hermitage are wisdom, kindness, and courage. If meeting is tough, deep, and tender enough then we can say with Lord Alfred Tennyson, "I am part of all I have met."

Our title, Spiritual Life Instance, says it all: "I come to give you life—abundant life" (Jesus). Boundless life! And this life of the Spirit is meant to be not in the first place institutionalized, but embodied and enjoyed in this instance, here and now.

The focus is not futuristic, idealistic, or moralistic. Though shaped in tradition, what count are creative engagement, mindful immersion, and a total response to the challenge and invitation of this instant. Moving (meeting) erotically, i.e. wholeheartedly, into the mystery of the other—the person, the dog, the tree, the project, the job, the illness or the ecstasy—that is the life stance of the embodied Spirit.

Imagine a family, a football team, a church, a school, a busy place of industry, a political party without fuss, lust, or rust. It would be a thing of beauty and, therefore, socially contagious. Justice and peace flow from such order. There would be an energetic ability *to be there*; plenty of time to be attentive, sensitive, and mindful. The result is a love-force that transforms the world—not all at once, of course, but ultimately if the lovers are faithful. And that takes courage because our shallow, secular lifestyle is against it. Ugliness prevails in our language, our movies, magazines, buildings, and the ubiquitous horror of litter and violence.

We need to strive for beauty. The wind resounds there. Revelation and elevation reside there. Nowhere are living flames of divinity so deliciously scorching and eternity so compelling. It is not the end but a plangent promise of the ultimate.

Life is dull, bland, and tedious without earth, sky, water, desert, and all of nature. Its massive onslaught and its scrumptiousness tease into the mystery beyond our senses. What is more shocking than sheer beauty? More riveting? More rapturous?

Earlier in this chapter, I say that the Trinity is the model of our universe, a communing of beings in one another rather than a collection of beings outside one another. The cosmos, a worldly relatedness of all of us, is an incarnation of the Trinity. "This is my body." Keiji Nishitani, in *Religion and Nothingness*, used two other words for the same thing: "circuminsessional interpenetration." And our own theological development today in terms of perichoresis—the divine dance—is a very important reference to God's Body as the wonderful interrelatedness of all beings.[6]

Only a few outstanding artists, authors, and movie directors have rendered the incomparable beauty of the sexual elements of lovemaking. Has there ever been a scene to match the Gospel love encounter between Jesus and the woman at the well? No nudity. No blatant sex. But this elemental force seethed in the entire atmosphere and thundered through every shimmering word.

Monastic life works only if it is very erotic and exquisitely pure. Celibates should be great lovers and so often they were. At this very time, the most prodigious lovers I know are celibate. Only mystics can be holy, happy celibates. And yet no one seems to face that in dealing with the recent[7] clergy crisis.

---

[6] See Beatric Bruteau, for instance, in *Cross Currents*, 1990.

[7] See the numerous cases of sexual misconduct and ecclesiastical cover-up.

Carmelites have always been dedicated to the mystical life and its development of mystical theology, an extremely arduous task; but think of Elijah and the saints who caught his gigantic spirit—and who is to back off into easier, softer ways? Our addiction to softness is monumental, but I can't deal with that here. An intense mystical life has never been more urgent. It is ecological, ecumenical, economical, eremitical, and the heart and soul of education and politics.

Not since the early centuries of the Church has Mystical Theology been the central teaching of the Mystical Body of Christ. Religious faith and doctrine have been atrociously affected by this lamentable lacuna. For instance, Catholic teaching on sexuality has been—and is now—a worldwide embarrassment. There is an absence of theological eros in the monasteries, convents, seminaries, universities, and parishes. Without religious-sexual integration, abuses abound.

Because Jesus was the holiest man to walk on the earth, he was also the sexiest. Religion should provide the healthiest Erosphere in the world. Then it would produce attractive saints.

The vows that bind Religious are the evangelical counsels that compel—suasively—lay people who follow Christ or Buddha or the Hebrew prophets. Poverty—pledging "no fuss"—is the first of evangelical imperatives. "No lust" is the second, which is the meaning of chastity. When our desire for communion

with the Ultimate unites and fructifies all our other desires, there remains but one hung, and no lust.

Freed of all interior clutter and external frenzy,
we are readied for the obediential experience of "no
rust": a clean, clear openness to revelation both traditional and spontaneous. Attentive now to God and his
world, we are bound to be astonished and ravished by
his awesome presence. *Obedire* means "to listen." We
must offer Love to the One who espouses us, here and
now, in this instance—a listening heart.

The Spiritual Life Instance has legal status, but
carefully avoids any Church/institutional denomina-
tion. This lay-ecumenical venture is on its own, though
blessed and honored by the Church—by its wise men
and women, who, responsible for necessary institutional embodiments and embellishments, realize how
absolutely important it is to foster the mystical life at
the center of the Church; and by paupers and prophets
who, for the sake of enlightened love, vigorously op-
pose what is conventionally prissy on the one hand,
and compulsively vulgar on the other.

The virtue that this lay, monastic foundation will
strive to cultivate to a remarkably high degree is Purity, which is undispersed energy. The personal passionate pursuit of the End—zeal for God, as Socrates
pointed out—will engage the lay monk in the most
erotic life on earth; cognitive and erotic, as he em-

phasized, precisely because it is the most comprehensive. In these depths, as in the dialogues of Plato, boundaries become so transparent they seem to disappear altogether.

The Greek *polis* weakened even the family bonds, confirming the possibility of an erotic life outside the family—an essential insight the Church has come to share. Lovers were swept beyond the limits of convention and law in assaying the experience of sex and exploring the broad possibilities of their own individuality. If monks eschew the risk and the hope of human connectedness embedded in eros, or if they envy or denigrate the high quality of sexual integration they notice in others, then they themselves are doomed and remain puppets of original sin, of radical un-love.

That's what Christ came to save us from. In other words, he became incarnate in order to transmit to us a spirit that will transfigure all of the flesh, that will put love where there is no love, leaving behind a legacy, a culture, an Erosphere at once contemplative and contagious, culminating in wholeness, holiness, and happiness.

To embody this fierce and fiery spirit, the monastic person cultivates a delicate language; to build the Erosphere, to meet mindfully, she treasures solitude. Seeking to be alone with God, he or she finds him at the heart of everything.

That is why some of the liveliest and sexiest human beings practice lay or religious monastic life; they do what the philosopher Spinoza suggested: "Make the body-mind do as many things as possible. This will perfect the whole mind and make us capable of an intellectual act of the love of God." It is metaphysically impossible to isolate aloneness with the cosmotheandric One. Love of the Ultimate means *aloneness*; this is *all-one-ness*.

When Frank Sheed told his wee son he needn't hide in the garage to be with God, that the Holy One was everywhere, the little fellow said, "I'm tired of an everywhere God. I want my God enfleshed, viscerally present—a unique, concrete, and incomparable experience." Stunned, Frank knew that here was a budding theologian.

Back to Plato. The splendid eroticism of Socrates makes pellucidly clear that this primary activity is always private. And universally, the erotic life will find its proper place within the discrete shelter of privacy. Within that sanctuary, more than anywhere else, one will find the coincidence of opposites, the union of polarities.

In that secret sexual ambiance, consciousness is heightened, the soul is enlivened. Spiritual growth is obvious, in fact, thrilling. In retrospect, a dirty mind, a scrupulous mind, an ignorant person may interject a motive that repudiates what in private was sheer worship—"with my body I thee worship."

There is nothing comparable to the transforming power of deep, profound, I-Thou encounters. But such charismatic meetings occur only between highly sexed and integrated persons. Our education in this area has failed us. Church seminaries have churned out professionals who, with their sacraments, compete with other professionals. But seldom are they God-intoxicated men, almost never great lovers.

Colleges train students to go on subverting Christianity so that they can focus on success. They usually become, as a result, self-made men, who indeed do worship their maker. Are monks any better? Do they make any difference? Are they sexually developed and integrated enough, are they Christ-formed enough, in love enough to engage unabashedly in their one valid apostolate—an inspired, personal, and precarious ministry among persons? Just how contemplative is the typical priest, nun, minister, or monk; and above all, parent, teacher, and lover?

This I-Thou experience is so important, my evaluation of my own lifetime work may help to clarify the nub of *apostolate*, a word I prefer to ministry, which is often nothing but a "mini-spree." Anyway, since 1950, I've had the privilege of establishing hermitages for apostolic hermits in the US, Canada, and Ireland, of teaching in five US universities, and preaching in every state.

I can only hope that this was helpful work. On the other hand, what I know helped in deep, life-changing, God-centered ways was the personal apostolate. The hundreds of letters I have received over more than half a century attest to a radical change of life, an ongoing religious experience and a taste of God.

What is it that happens here when two people truly meet? *Eros* happens—an erotic explosion of divine life and love. Eros means *care*—full of awe, reverence, wonder and worship. From these depths—beyond words, clichés, and slogans; free of sham, categories, or boundaries; attached to neither history nor symbols—rises the Spirit, a force and fiery presence, an awesome energy who comes not to coo but to wow; not to comfort but to conduct us into the fire. Once delusion turns to ashes, we will be free—no more craving, no more aversion. We are now nothing but loving.

When lovers meet, they soul-friend one another. Each ego shrinks in the presence of sacred otherness. The unknown depth of the other is carefully explored. Discovery, as Jesus taught, is the Kingdom come. Their encounter is awesome, tender, and affectionate; and yet, detached. It is not silly or sappy, but salient. It is not romantic but monastic. The spiritual experience is indispensable. It may eventuate in matrimonial capers or mystical raptures, but in either case a serious commitment is also indispensable. Broken vows—

marital or religious, or even between friends—equals defection, which is extremely serious.

There is only one way to respond to the absolute and that is absolutely. Of course, if one partner goes berserk, what can the other do? But the Ground of Being is unberserkable. So!

The meetings of all of us are unlike those between clients and their lawyers, therapists, and religious professionals, or even ecclesiastical apparatchiks. Real meetings are more like that between Jesus and the Samaritan woman at the well, or between the Lord and Mary Magdalen, or his beloved disciple John, or between Saint Francis and Saint Clare, or Jeanne de Chantal, or the extraordinary life of Abelard and Heloise. When members of religious orders take vows, they wed the community, the place, and the Spirit embodied there.

The hermitage is not a rest home for tired people, but a vortex of vital, valiant seekers of ultimate reality, and of the freedom such a deep endeavor requires of us. This is no flight from the world, but from the noise, frenzy, endless talk, mindless feverish activities; the dull collective routines of popular, trivial pietistic pursuits; and the inauthentic self, lost in the vast emptiness of the public mind. Such a vacuous pseudo existence adjusts one to "mass man" but alienates the human being. We live in an alien culture. To some degree each of us is alienated from him or herself. We desperately need solitude in which we learn to be still and to see how infinitely attractive God is. By his beauty we are smitten, and by his intimate presence we are overwhelmed.

Twenty years from now our psychological tests will be a joke; our "treatment" will seem trite, trendy, and woefully unsophisticated. The questions we ask should be jubilantly tolerant of eccentricities; at the same time, however, sparing others of our own fatuous inanities. Prayerfulness and playfulness underlie one's whole exciting adventure. Relatedness—human, animal, and vegetable—abounds with attention riveted at the center of the cosmotheandric Presence.

This ravishing astonishment satisfies the personal passionate yearning for intimate union with the Ultimate Spouse—yours and mine. After all, to the Origin, the Source, the Holy One, all the world is wedded.

Everyone knows this saying of Shakespeare: "To be or not to be, that is the question." St. Thomas Aquinas shed even more light: "To be is to be *with* (esse est coesse)." Martin Buber makes his assertion with brio: "All life is meeting." Let me, as their batboy, say my piece: "To meet or not to meet; *that* is the question."

Each one is talking about "the one thing necessary," which is the Mystical Life. So Karl Rahner, the most lucid modern theologian, asserts in so many words, that if we do not soon become mystics—lured by the shocking beauty and terrible truth—well, then, we are out of Schlitz.[8] The center cannot hold. Society is now a mass of compulsions and convulsions.

John, author of the fourth Gospel, was right, of course. But the rest of Scripture elucidates his unadorned proclamation: "In the beginning was the Word." Divine Revelation unpacks it by insisting, "In the beginning was silence," the matrix of the Word, the mother of meaning. The Word can be meaningful, transforming our lives, only if we are silent and solitary enough. Stillness is the secret. Psalm 46 says it all: "Be still and know that I am God." Achieve that, sustain that, and our techno-barbaric juggernaut will be stopped; the dehumanization of man will cease.

I look for five qualities in a contemplative lay monk or "nunk[9]": a quest for life, a stretch of mind, a love of Christ, a sense of humor, and an endless, boundless wonder. This would preclude narcissism,

---

[8] A brand of beer.

[9] Through the millennia, both men and women have lived monastic lives. Living and worship locations for men have been called "monasteries"; those for women, "convents." Men in such cases are referred to as monks, whereas women are referred to as nuns. In a few instances, a monastery was located near a convent though neither was coed. "Nunk" was coined by one of McNamara's communities to refer to a woman leading a monastic life on par with that of monks. The contemplative communities founded by McNamara under the Spiritual Life Institute (not to be confused with the later Spiritual Life Instance) were coed, but each monk and nunk lived in a separate hermitage.

pettiness, and perfectionism—three big obstacles to authentic being.

The diminished culture of the world and the derivative nature of our shallow, uprooted society seep—thanks to the secular media and religious apathy—into our monastic enclaves. And we sell out. Instead of following Christ—and I recently heard a smarmy, know-it-all religious superior condemn such fidelity to the Gospels—we support the imperatives of a contemporary, modern culture of alienation. We have utterly secular minds with a few spiritual patches. So we settle down in the empire and pretend to be pioneers of the Kingdom.

Lord save us or we perish.

So do we need religion? Yes, if it ignites, preserves, and enjoys the experiential awareness of the Ineffable: the pure and direct intuition of God born of love. Religion without religious experience is a corpse. Unfortunately, as the philosopher Santayana put it with pellucid clarity, "Having forgotten the end, we multiply the means." This leaves us with a subverted Christianity and an inflated institution. To a large extent, we are being fed stones instead of bread.

Despite a massive dissatisfaction with the institution of religion—which has today acquired a negative connotation, even an obstacle to the fundamental experience of faith—so many people are saying, "I have a spiritual life; I don't need religion." Such private, individualistic spiritualties are no better than fossilized institutions. Without luscious dogmas and lively doctrines, our spirit languishes. Religion is a constitutive dimension of being human.

We are social animals and therefore need to be inspired by, and respond to, the onslaught of God's love in socially appropriate ways. The institution is immensely helpful when the means of worship reach their end—awareness of the Ineffable—when its public practice preserves the primordial religious experience and makes it accessible to all. It mush eschew moralism and set the stage for high moral acts.

Religion sanctifies to the extent that it is thin, slim, transparent and utterly open; clinging to the basic deposit of faith without becoming stiff, stuffy, and stagnant. Only if the Church shares and expresses the consciousness of Christ can it be holy and produce saints. To serve the human process, the Church must be supple and flexible. Otherwise, there is no transformation in Christ.

Besides, when you gather together the People of God to do the one thing necessary, to share what they most prize, extraordinary events and edifices are often the uplifting results. They become concrete memoirs of divine-human encounters, and compellingly attractive invitations to leap above and beyond the boring frippery and fatuous inanities of everyday pseudo existence.

Just to cite a few examples, there's the Vatican, Notre Dame, Chartres, Santa Sophia, the Taj Mahal; the great monasteries, glorious places such as Assisi and Lourdes. Oh, and here's one to stoke your fire: The largest, liveliest crowd of enthusiastic young people gathered on the streets of Denver, Colorado. Why? To see Pope John Paul II. Finally, how significant that the World's most treasured art is religious.

Beauty is incomparable, but it's promise, not a fulfillment. Despite some ugly aberrations—warring, lusting, and ruling way beyond its wisdom and authority—the religious promise remains cogent and seductive.

The beauty of the Spiritual Life Instance (SLInstance), full of promise, appealed to the hierarchy. Let me share with you some responses to the birth and growth of the Spiritual Life Instance. The upward movement was from institute (the Spiritual Life Institute was founded in 1960) to instance (SLInstance was founded in 2004), from experiment to experience. The episcopal evaluation was euphoric.

Bishop Austin Burke, Halifax, Nova Scotia:

"My most fervent prayer was for a community just like what Friar McNamara has here in my diocese—a contemplative community of apostolic hermits. Their silent witness and salutary work is so impressive."[10]

Bishop Finnegan, Ireland:

"I consider the most effective thing God inspired me to do in my diocese of Mayo in Ireland was to invite and help to establish this canonical community of young, vibrant apostolic hermits. Their life, based on the ancient Rule of the Carmelite Order, is ideal for here and now."[11]

Cardinal George Flahiff, Canada:

"No light has burnt like this one since the Celtic monasticism of Kevin, Kieran, and the Columbans. Very much like Bridget and Brendan....God be with this lively bunch of monks and nuns (sic)."

---

[10] Nova Nada was founded in 1972. In 1997, the monastic community moved away due to intensive logging by a forestry corporation. Despite many meetings, no accommodation to the life of prayer and silence was granted to the community. The site remains a retreat center, however, and carries on as Birchdale Lake. In 2011, Birchdale celebrated the 100th anniversary of the site's founding.

[11] Holy Hill was established in 1995 as one of the Spiritual Life Institute's monastic communities. Following the dissolution of Nova Nada, the Institute was split between Crestone, Colorado ("Nada") and Holy Hill in Skreen, County Sligo, Ireland. In 2016 they changed their name to the Carmelite Community of Apostolic Hermits.

Cardinal John Wright, Rome:

"What this young community, founded by Pope John (XXIII) and Fr. William McNamara in 1960, has already, by the grace of God, achieved, is remarkable. Believing that action without contemplation is blind, it focuses on the one thing necessary. Following Christ and the mystics of all the holy traditions into awareness of the Ineffable—reliving the ancient Rule of Carmel in creative, contemporary ways—promises fathomless depths for a society whose deep down longing is for ultimate joy; for God, who is Love."

Bishop Paul Dudley, South Dakota:

"Fr. William McNamara led two of our diocesan retreats. For the first and only time, all of our priests—conservative and liberal—had a positive and enjoyable response, accepting his deep spiritual challenge gladly. The community of Apostolic Hermits is contemplative and shares its experience of God in deep, pure human relationships. A personal, loving friendship is the perfect love of God. Trust and endurance characterize both."

Cardinal Cushing, Boston, Massachusetts:

"I knew something would happen when Pope John XXIII and Father William got together, and that something may turn out to be the most important event of the twentieth century. I'm glad I helped to arrange the meeting in 1960."

Contemplation in Action

Finally, besides being contemplative, the Church must engage in action—action that is discriminating and selective. In other words, inspired. Just as action without contemplation is blind, so contemplation without action is taradiddle, a blunted narrow outlook on life expressed in a flatulent flurry of words, words, words.

Religious action is not fustian but combustion, an evolutionary process, spiritual not chemical, where hundreds of thousands of disciplined men and women produce an interior heat and light that would not otherwise be at our personal disposal and enlarges our capacity for transforming society.

What we need in church is admiration and expectation—something terrifyingly and joyfully new, unspeakably fresh and gloriously overwhelming. After all, we are about to face the absolute, the ultimate. Absolute may be the wrong word. Better to say, "The absolutely loving one." Otherwise, we bring our sameness, our dullness, and our boredom to a sacred place of worship. If the ministers, priests, or chairmen—famous or funny—are not on the same wavelength as God, what hope is there? We shouldn't imitate TV personalities; we must "put on the mind of Christ."

Real life is experiential. And takes two fundamental forms: an external empiricism, namely science; and an internal empiricism, namely mysticism. We need both, especially mysticism. It springs from the deepest human level. It is also more certain than science. But like science, full of revelatory surprises, especially at heaven's gate:

You present your jolly managerial self. "Here I am, Pete—Glad to join you, Pal. I'm sure you need help."

"But you cannot come in."

"What? I built the cockamamie towers. And I'm number one headhunter."

"I know. I read it in the Saphein (sic) comic book. Look over there, my friend. Who can fit through that very small door?"

"A small child or a dog. Oh no! Is that the only door?"

"I'm afraid so, dear Captain of Industry. Only little ones with childlike spirit or humble dogginess can enter heaven."

So!

When traveling, I go to Mass. I detect no ardent participation, no serious commitment, no ecstasy, no hunger for divine union, no obvious Lover's Touch felt and fecund. No metanoia, no radical transformation.[12] Skip also the unctuous twaddle at the front

---

[12] At my own parish, I have observed several double-parked cars—as if the drivers were certain they would be able to get

door of the church. It spoils the mood. People don't go to church for ever more trivial, everyday stuff. God is not a mascot or an uncle; the Holy One, the Ineffable evokes wonder, awe, dread and delight. The beginning of wisdom is fear—not psychological fear but ontological humility. As the biblical poet said, "Be still and see that God is God."

Since we are human and God is surprise, the funniest things happen in church as well as solemn worship. Take for example, the First Communion boy returning to his pew, rubbing his tummy with sheer delight and lit up with the happiness of the cherubim. Or the night I, a crippled preacher, so sitting rather than standing, got carried away—first, by speaking too long, then again when suddenly two priests came from behind, lifted me up, and carried me away a second time.

Oh, a dramatic, uproarious case! Friar Paul, small in stature and ebullient in spirit, asked for a stool to be placed behind the pulpit. I found one just right, though on wheels. Paul mounted it with royal dignity. But with his first wild gesture, the stool began to slide. The endangered priest began to yell, barroom style. All the way across the sanctuary. Waving in maniacal fashion and embarrassed, he kept his balance until he hit the opposite wall. He was magnificent.

---

out early, unscathed, and rush home as if it had been a normal day. How sad that Mass—our sacramental encounter with the Trinity—has become so tame.

Another day at the same mission I was preaching about the intrinsic dignity and holiness of a cat, the feline embodiment of God. At that very moment came a bodacious cat, bathed in splendid ambience, with all the adroit maneuvers of Aslan[13] or Metro-Goldwyn-Mayer's lion. No one was going to intercept her majestic confrontation with the Godhead. And so she bellowed. The walls rattled. The pews rocked, the silly men stood still, stuck in fright. The feline beauty resumed her original stride up the aisle, up the steps and onto the very altar of Divinity, of flaming love. By now the crowd had regained its gormless sangfroid. "Father, she's on the altar. Help!" The Beloved longed for her to be there. The ultimate meeting between lovers. Who am I to dare profane this ravishment? (A true story[14])

Here is an even more spectacular one. A bishop, myself, and one hundred other folks gathered outside the church by a lovely lake, with lots of ducks and a blue heron. Sublimity. Time for Communion. The bishop lifted the Host from the ciborium to put on the

---

[13]See C.S. Lewis's series the Chronicles of Narnia for descriptions of Christ as Aslan, who "was not a very tame lion."

[14] In accordance with his Irish roots, McNamara weaves a good yarn. I leave them as found in the manuscript. I leave the reader with this caution: Once he claimed to have swum with loons—those hauntingly beautiful but very skittish birds. My doubts were dashed when he dove into Lake Winnipesaukee and two loons appeared out of nowhere and swam very near and around him until he emerged from the lake as if the whole encounter was the most normal thing possible.

tongue of Nora McK. That's when it happened: Quick as can be, a duck ran lickety-split to that awful rendezvous and snapped the consecrated bread from the bishop's hand and ran off with his catch, quite proud of himself. (A true story)

Just one more. Honestly, a final true story. I hate jokes. Human folly is so much funnier: This church had a fine program for bringing Communion to the sick. The church had a special tabernacle with a front and back door, so no matter if a priest was celebrating Mass, one could access the sacrament unseen without creating a disturbance. One night, Father Joe got the call to deliver Communion to the sick. So he went to the back door of the tabernacle and opened it just as Father Tim, a very devout man, was about to close the door on his side. As was Father Tim's pious custom, assuming he and Jesus were alone, he said, "Goodnight Jesus." And Father Joe said, "Goodnight, Tim." Well, imagine the next impious meeting between Joe and Tim. Oh, did Tim wax eloquent about the "miracle" and hearing Jesus's voice.

I meant to write about the Church in action, holiness made present on the streets, in the schools, in Hollywood, government, marketplace, families and sports. But the canine, feline, ducky forms of God got me. Creator and creature are not identical but enjoy a union so intimate it is sometimes hard to tell one from the other.

The oldest, surest doctrine of Christianity is not pantheism, but pan*en*theism. God is the bear but the bear is not God. When a wild bear looked into my eyes and I petted him, I could not separate them[15]. But I knew even then that they were distinct. Same for us, of course. But we have trouble being our true selves. Swollen egos get in the way. Only our divine lover can completely reduce the ego. Only the source of being, the principle of order, can woo and draw us into freedom, though that does not mean we can do whatever we want; rather, it means we can do, and gladly so, whatever it takes to be authentic in Christ. We need a few things at the same time: wisdom, a taste for the right things; the courage to do and to protect those right things; and finally, to be faithful to that commitment.

My brother is ninety years old, his wife close behind.[16] Even to this day, they are the most romantic couple I know. Very erotic. Remember the Greek word *eros* means care. That is why those ancient saints close to Christ—Origin, Ignatius, and Gregory of Nyssa—found the words God and *Eros* interchangeable. And rightly so.

I call my brother Bill and his wife, Kay, erotic because of the exquisite care between them as well as for

---

[15] In Oregon, a bear was eating plums straight from McNamara's favorite tree. He left the safety of his hermitage to instruct the bear…

[16] This portion was written in 2012.

all their friends, including a few versions of Christ in his most disreputable form. Such magnanimity and magnificence! Un-canonized saints are some of the best, thank God.

Saints—touched sinners—keep the world from falling apart. A deep profound culture issues from their lively being, their infectious presence. They seem capable of incomparable feats *en route* to the numinous.

They remind me of my favorite author, Nikos Kazanzakis:

"I am a bow in your hand, Lord
Draw me lest I rot.
Do not overdraw me, Lord
Lest I break.
Overdraw me, Lord and who
Cares if I break."

A perfect summation of spiritual growth. The opposite of subverted Christianity.

The Shape of Monastic Life

How many people know that the first book in English was written by Saint Julian of Norwich, a female hermit?

Great literature and a rich culture were preserved in the world by monks. And I suspect it will be the monks who will save society from secularism. Right now, we live on the cusp of the monastic moment. We will find, on both a private and public level, the gradual replacement of society's sickness; namely softness, shallowness, and selfishness. Simultaneously men and women, especially youth, will shed their attachment to subverted Christianity and begin to follow Christ. Or rather follow Jesus, the most manly man, further and further into the deep mystery that underlies all being, permeates every human situation. This is an exquisitely human way of becoming like Jesus, the contemporary Christ. No more subverted, domesticated Christianity, but authentic Christ-ness. If a senator is not holy, he or she is unfit to be a senator. If a golfer does not pray an hour every day, she is goofy. If a monk doesn't pray six hours a day, he should be suspect.

The vivacious Episcopalian Bishop Desmond Tutu said, "I am so busy I cannot afford to pray for less than two hours a day."

The deepest human impulse is monastic. No one is happy without God. Remember, though, that means God is even closer than you are to yourself or to your spouse. A church in action is above all a church in prayer—an unfathomable cry of the heart. Why "cry"? Because they are wounded by the fierce and fiery Holy Spirit. Who can grasp the totality of that?

This is holiness no matter where you are or what you are doing. It's infectious. So be there. That's enough. The Deity's name is the Lord, [17] which means "The One who is always there." We are the image and the likeness of God so being there is our primordial essence. Our absence is our downfall. Fullness of life is in all situations personal, passionate presence. Contemplation is taking a long, loving look at the real. The basic human impulse is monastic— seeking first the kingdom of God. Awareness of the Ineffable. Adoration.

We need religiousness more than ever. Not the Establishment of religion, but docility to the Spirit in every walk of life.

Spiritual Life Instances Practices

1. One hour of meditation and prayer between 6:00 a.m. and 9:00 a.m.

2. One hour of meditation and prayer between 5:00 p.m. and 10:00 p.m.
   These practices take place in solitude, but we pray together at Mass on Wednesdays and on Sundays at 9:00 a.m.

3. Divisions of chores are discussed once a month.

---

[17] Out of respect for our Jewish friends we substitute "the Lord" for the Holy Name.

4. Preserve a silent, solitary, and leisurely atmosphere.
5. Cultivate an Erosphere (love one another).
6. Formal dress for formal sessions in the chapel. Prayer robes are available.
7. Take God seriously, but everything else with reverent lightness.
8. Play as much as possible and work leisurely, mindfully, not excessively.
9. No good ruts. And no bad ones either. But I worry more about the good ones.
10. Do something wild every day.
11. Silence.

This Rule of Life has no rigidities. It encourages essential behavior minimized, if not nullified, by both a secular society and a subverted Christianity. It does not aim at rectitude, but at amplitude. And that, Jesus said, is why he came; not to perform and depart, but to remain and *impart* the Spirit.

My Vocation
1. To live fully and selflessly.
2. To become a contemplative, ravished by God.
3. To disabuse myself and others of the illusion of already being a Christian.
4. To convey Christ, i.e. to cast fire.

5. To restore the human, God-centered centrality of life.

True Religion[18]

John the Scot, a neglected ninth century theologian, was probably the best and soundest Christian
thinker between Augustine and Thomas Aquinas. Ap-
pealing to Saint Augustine, John contends with un-
blinking certitude that true religion is true philosophy[19]
and, conversely, that true philosophy is true religion.

Faith focused on scripture lies at the beginning of
the Christian's religious inquiry; yet if error is to be
avoided, scripture must be interpreted in harmony
with reason. Faith is itself the principle from which
knowledge of the Creator begins to develop. Faith of
its nature kindles in the mind an intellectual light
which is none other than that of philosophy (love of
wisdom, hunger, a taste for the right things).

John brought to the West and southward the way
of thought initiated by Pseudo-Dionysius the Areopa-
gite and Maximus the Confessor. His interpretation of
biblical texts is more reasonable and less allegorical
than the extravagant expositions of Saint Ambrose

---

[18] McNamara's notes indicate that the following essay was to
be incorporated into this chapter. It is presented here without
any effort at a complete integration. Obviously, though, if we
do indeed need religion, what form might that take?
[19] Taken literally, "philosophy" means "a love of wisdom."

and Saint Augustine. It's hardly accidental that the best philosophers—or should I say my favorites—conveyed an intense mystical element and were, in fact, in so many cases, veritable mystics. From Plato to E. I. Watkin, they are legion.

As Watkin says in *Philosophy of Mysticism*, without mysticism religion is a corpse, and culture, a monstrosity. He insists that all of us bear at least the lower levels of mystical experience within us, and that for culture:

> The mystics are the advanced guard of the army of the elect. They are the spies who have gone on ahead and entered before death into the Promised Land to report somewhat of it to their fellow travelers in the desert. For proof they bring us back a cluster of grapes such as never grew in the vineyards of Egypt.

The other great theologian and mystical guide of the twentieth century was Baron von Hugel[20]. With

---

[20] Wikipedia (accessed December 13, 2017) has it that Friedrich von Hugel was born in 1852 in Florence and died in London in 1925. He wrote numerous books and was a correspondent with John Henry Newman among other influential thinkers and religious leaders. He was awarded honorary degrees by the University of St. Andrews and the University of Oxford, despite having been a self-taught biblical scholar. Among his most well-known works is *The Mystical Element*

typical incisiveness he pointed out the three constitutive elements of religion: institutional, intellectual, and mystical. Of these the mystical is first and foremost. Nothing is more obvious in the history of humankind than the equation between the high levels of mysticism and the high times of humanity. This is even more obvious in the Church. When mysticism is rife the Church is full of life.

During this transitional age of shallow, horizontal extremities, the Church needs more than ever to recover its vertical lift into the deep, enlivening mystical life of Christ (who embodies the whole Mystery, and intimately reveals the Beyond in our midst.) Only this level of contemplation will renew the love life of the Church. A Church divinely infected becomes a contagion. Apart from that contagion, a flaunted "modern ministry" is nothing but a mini-spree. Maybe that's what Rome worries and warns us about[21]; not a collaborative laity, but *unsent* apostles. We need to be called, or rather, to recognize the call (vocation[22]), to be touched, or rather, to be aware of the touch at the core of our being (contemplation), and then to be sent, or better, to be lured by God into the ministry (apostle means to be sent). The active one here is God. The

---

of Religion: As Studied in Saint Catherine of Genoa and Her Friends, 2 volumes.

[21] Particularly during the pontificate of Benedict XVI.

[22] "Vocation" comes from the Latin, *vocare*, "to call."

responsive and, therefore, responsible one is the religious or lay minister.

God sends no one—neither priest nor lay person—into ministry unless he or she has already begun to be transformed. Not finished! If we think we are finished, well, we are—indeed! Since we cannot give what we do not have, what God and the contextual situation require of us is contemplative action, an ardent and arduous love life shared. In other words, personal, passionate presence is what characterizes a lovely, lively person and a vital, vigorous Church.

Despite the present deformity of the Church and the desolation of the culture, there will be more life than ever in the Church and more beauty and brilliance in the culture. If we move swiftly and serenely through this dark and lucky night, we will discover the astonishing presence of the Pure and Holy One whom we have not trivialized. This is no God in the gaps, but in the deeps, beyond our pious machinations.

The deadness of the Church is not a new phenomenon. It is rather a newly noticeable modern form of vacuity. It began in its essential form in the seventeenth and eighteenth centuries when the Church repudiated its mystical life, its raison d'être, and behaved more like an organization than the Mystical Body of Christ, a transparent organ of vision, love and life, a vehicle of the Numinous.

What we need to do now, as the heavy, outward ecclesiastical stuff collapses, is move deliberately and delightfully inside the Mystery and receive what God infinitely desires to give: the manifestation of the Godhead, Ultimate Reality. We are sick of instruction. We want manifestation, contemplation, divine vision. We must not skip instruction but make it connect with revelation—the God-centered experience of I-Thou encounters. This is a holy worldliness—a perceptive appreciation of things as they really are; a long, loving look at the real. Our creed, laws, and doctrines are no more than pointers to the Reality "in which we live, move, and have our being."

Purity is undiminished energy. When we are no longer distracted by trivia, scandalized by sin, or enslaved by means—the media of Church and State—we can do the one thing necessary and offer to God our pure hearts. The mystical life is the life of sinners touched by the merciful God. It is not esoteric, it is not even difficult; "my yoke is easy, my burden is light." We—organizational men and women—complicate the simple life of loving awareness and humble service.

Obviously the soul needs release from itself and desires it more than anything. It longs for a life and meaning, for a power greater than itself, which is found perfectly in union with God. "Modern man's" need for religion is enormous. That a relatively sane society cannot endure without religion—in school, church, family, and government (i.e. the *virtue* of religion fostered by a separate Church whose chief business is to sanctify politics as well as everything else)—is clearly evident. What makes this blatantly obvious is the destructive and insane state of the first radically secular civilization in history—first America and now, egregiously, Ireland.[23]

Morality is one thing, and important enough I am now talking about a larger issue of which morality is a by-product. I am addressing an issue larger than the Church. Religion, properly understood, relates us to the roots of life, the ground (or better, the *ungrund*—underground) of being. Without this we do not know what it feels like to be alive. We are deprived of meaning, and purpose alone turns us into robots. Without religion we feel that reality itself is an inane vacuum, a chaos, in which we create purely artificial and make-believe meanings out of our own heads. Along with this, precisely because we are so basically good and naturally religious, we feel our own sham and humbug and so we anticipate our ultimate frustration. This explains drunkenness, despair, and the appalling increase in suicides. Even uprooted sex loses its luster; i.e. sex without love, awe, reverence, and humor.

Absorbed in the creation of artificial meanings it is possible, for a while, to forget reality, though the sense

---

[23] This essay was initially written in response to an article appearing in the *Irish Independent* (newspaper).

of futility remains as an undertone of feeling breaking out into consciousness in times of crisis. At such times we *know* our desperate need for religion (and its institutions); at others we only feel it as an unexplained void in the heart.

So many seem enamored of "short-term commitments," the very thing that has turned the playful glory of sports into an ugly business. According to Dr. Clare, an outstanding Irish psychiatrist, "A lifetime commitment, be it to God or to Intel, is not part of the zeitgeist!" There you have it—the modern mood caught lugubriously in one casual sentence. Add to that his dubious proclamation that the "power of the institutional church is utterly spent." We'll see. I am a hermit, and therefore no institutional man with love of the establishment. But you can't have an orchestra, a ball game, or a church without an institution. It should be slim, transparent, and in the background, but without it not much happens and nothing endures.

There is one essential thing without which human life is meaningless. That one thing is mystical life (a loving awareness and direct union with God). The divine life is what the Church embodies in her institutions, doctrines, and liturgy. Such life exists outside of these chief conductors but is extremely hard to get at, though some saints and heroes do, as do devout Hindus, Buddhists, Moslems, and Jews, to mention four of the great religions.

The Church is ashamed of its grumpy rectitude. It is grateful for its Christian amplitude—Catholic and Protestant versions. All it strives for is more and more life. To live is to love and to love is to die. That's it. The present low ebb of Church religion consists in the fact that rarely, even for Church people, does it give the soul any knowledge of union with the reality that underlies the universe. There is no Christ-consciousness, no felt-presence of the Holy One. Not *feelings* mind you, but the awestruck person in the direct presence of the Ineffable God. If the Church is not mystical enough, it is not fully and essentially religion.

A personal, passionate awareness of the Holy One, the realization of one's union with God, in a word, mysticism or contemplation, is not merely the flowering of religion. It is absolutely necessary. Christian faith and practice have lost force because the majority of Christians, both devout and nominal, do not know what "God" means. We know a bit about Jesus and we remember Patrick, Colmcille, and Brigit. But we have no experiential knowledge of the Love who empowered and intoxicated them. If we merely imitate them, even their ideas, we are engaged in monkey business.

Chapter Two

Pilgrim of the Absolute[24]

Monk[25] and pilgrim are synonymous. Both have one, single, motivating reason for everything they do and that reason is Christ. Life is following Christ, a freely chosen way that is creative, imaginative, and unique; a way that is always brand new and always biblical. How prevalent is this truly human way in monastic life today?

This is a good time for the reader to put down this book for a while and read Ken Follett's *The Pillars of the Earth*. It is the best novel I've read[26] in years. One of the things it does is portray monastic life in the Middle Ages in a shockingly realistic way. Monks

---

[24] This chapter, with some modification, first appeared as an article in *Communio*, 24, 1997. "The Monk as Passionate Pilgrim of the Absolute."

[25] "Monk" comes from the Greek "*monos,*" meaning "one" or "alone."

[26] McNamara writes, "With the assistance of books on tape for the blind."

then, as now, highlight the glory and folly of human existence. Monasteries today, as then, are often absurdly antithetical to the Gospel. Constant renewal is required to prevent the slippery slide into absurdity. The root of "absurd" is *surdus*, Latin for "deaf." The pathetic plight of society—monasteries as well—comes from the inability to hear <u>directly and immediately</u> the Word of God.

Whoever recovers this ability is a pure monk. To such a listening heart, God speaks. The monk absorbs, assimilates, and embodies the Word and, in turn, speaks. Such a one, God's beloved monk, is the message. So as not to wear out the word "monk" I will use in this book the synonym "pilgrim," the one who seeks one joy and is grateful to any creature of any experience that points the way to the One whose felt presence is absolute joy.

The pilgrim of the Absolute is one who responds absolutely to the summons of the Absolute. The pilgrim is ravished by the Holy One who addresses every human being in the world. God addresses each one of us singly, uniquely, and undividedly even as he unites us together as his People, his Church. He takes the initiative, he hallows, sanctifies, and fulfills—all so very freely, in cooperation with a free human response.

The pilgrim is one who perceives how Absolute Love—not something static but the swirling sheerness of Being—addresses him or her in everyday life, in all relationships and events, in every concrete, contextual situation. Perceiving how we are called, moved, sent, is the contemplative act. Without contemplation— that pure, simple intuition of the Ultimate born of love, that capacity, indeed longing, for intimate communion, that long, loving look at the Real—without that, there is no perceptive appreciation of being called, touched, sent. Let me be brave and say it: without contemplative perception there is no vocation. That may be the human tragedy at the outset of the twenty-first century. If there is no perceived vocation, there is no meaningful existence. That is why, except for the holy ones, we all "live quiet lives of desperation."[27]

We must not be fooled by the racket we make; scratch the noisy surface of modern life and a despair as quiet and final as death overwhelms us. The twentieth century was a century of death—more violence, suicides included, than any other century. So much for progress! Malcolm Muggeridge claimed that the twentieth century will be remembered, above all else, for its death wish, expressed ferociously and lubriciously in all its forms of megalomania and erotomania.

---

[27] Thoreau.

The very institutions meant to correct this sinful tendency toward death have ended up aiding and abetting the downward transcendence toward power, profit, and pleasure. In so doing they rob us of the ability, even the taste for, upward transcendence toward glory: becoming so deified in our distinctively human lives that we are pleasing to God. There is no comparable human pleasure, no other happiness.

The Place of Leisure

In this regard, two institutions are remarkable for their failure: the schools and the churches. The Greeks invented *skoles* to provide places of leisure for the people. That is what *skole*—school—means: a place where people could be still and be guided by skillful masters into experiential wisdom. The visionary Greeks also knew that "without vision the people perish" (Proverbs 29:18), that the most important thing to do is *to be*, that leisurely activity is so good in itself, so intrinsically worthwhile, that it needs no justification outside of itself. In leisure—school settings when they are right—there is no frenzied tempo, no scramble for grades or for success, no competition. Neither is there mental vacuity, laziness, or idleness.[28]

---

[28] Over coffee and stollen this afternoon, my hosts and I were discussing different forms of universities. In Germany, for example, students read material on their own and then participate in discussions with their professor and other students.

There is the supreme pleasure of a mind wholly acti-
vated, totally engaged, wisely passive and fully possessed, alert and at rest. Revelation occurs because a
person in leisure, in school, gathers together all of the
fragmented, distracted forces of personal being into
a unified magnet of attention, of recollection. This is
the purpose of schools. The information highway
leads elsewhere.

The churches have failed as well, and in a major way, similar to the schools. A distinguished group
of businessmen went on a long retreat recently for the
explicit purpose of designating the single overriding
need of contemporary society. The conclusion they
agreed on was this: the single overriding need of contemporary society is to rediscover, celebrate, and incarnate the sacred. Here we have a very secular group
recognizing the centrality of the sacred, and the dire
need to enflesh it in everyday life.

That is how we become pilgrims of the Absolute. By affirming the inherent sacredness of things,
we hallow them—everything, every person and place,
every community, all activities, and all creatures. The
churches, however, are meant to provide a specially

There are no formal lectures as in America. This European
style of instruction forces each student to gain a certain level
of mastery on his or her own rather than merely memorizing
what was said in class. Such studies require a very different
kind of commitment from the students.

sacred place for us to become sacred ourselves as we experience personally and passionately the Sacred Presence, the Holy One. By this real encounter with the Living God we become "Goddened," divinized. The Lord of the universe makes this declaration over the bread and wine, over all of us, over the totality of being, over the scabrously raw matter of the world: This is my body. Our response: Amen, indeed. This is the heart of the mystery; the *mysterium tremendum* and the *mysterium fascinans*. Since Rudolf Otto, thousands of us have used these words[29]. Rightly so. Even though Latin, the words jump out at us. They are gravid with meaning; primordial words that capture the central mystery of faith. At this center we enjoy simultaneously the passionate pitch of transcendence and the compassionate plunge into immensity.

But do we really? The divine address is there all right. But how much response? Address and response, I-Thou, meeting—this is the essence of religion. How present am I? How disposed? How vulnerable? How poor, naked, and hungry? How human a man's or woman's Eucharistic amen? Saint Thomas Aquinas said that's the key question: how humanly— "perfectly"—do we participate?

---

[29] Rudolf Otto (1869-1937) wrote *The Idea of the Holy* from which this phrase comes. "Terrible mystery" and "fascinating mystery" (Brittanica.com and referenceworks.brillonline.com, accessed December 15, 2017).

The point I want to make here is that the churches fail to provide a sufficiently sacred atmosphere—one full of silence, awe, wonder, mystery and glory. I hesitate to use the best of all words because it has been plundered by kooks and spooks. The word is prayer. Here it may be enough to say that prayer is a cry of the heart—the sacred sinner's heart. The theology underlying that particular description of prayer will also be found elsewhere.[30]

Here I simply want to repudiate all forms of *Kirchenschlaf*, a German word that captures the sour solemnity and grim gravity of so much behavior in church. The funniest things happen in church. Men and women of prayer notice and enjoy these happy blunders or inspired gaffes almost as much as God does. I am always thrilled when dogs and cats join us in church. They keep us young at heart.

I miss the old introductory prayer for Mass: "I will go to the altar of God; to God the joy of my youth." It was a plea for God's youthfulness in us. So much better than the false note often struck by the chatty "good morning" or even by the proper liturgical greeting when pronounced unctuously or carelessly.

---

[30] See William McNamara, *Earthy Mysticism*, (New York: Crossroad Publishing Co., 1983) 25-38; idem, *Christian Mysticism*, (Rockport, Massachusetts: Element, 1981), 146-154; and idem, *Forefront*, (Spring 1996), 30.

Just as the school's chief obligation is to establish a carefully structured time and place of leisure, so the church's big responsibility is not simply to get the people to church but, in church, to offer the people a terrible beauty, a truth clothed in splendor and a palpable love. A church that does this does not cater to a dull and dreary pietism, a soft and shallow devotionalism, or finally, a respectable mediocrity.

What the Church proffers is both an invitation and a challenge to enter into the sacred presence of the Holy One. This is like going into the cave of a lion. Who knows if we will come out alive? "The beginning of wisdom is fear" say the Scriptures. Not neurotic anxiety but ontological humility. Real fear, awe, fosters not priggish pygmies of the absurd but passionate pilgrims of the Absolute. What plagues the pilgrim is prettiness, what pulls and prods to the end is beauty. Small pleasures must not be scorned, but they must not stall the one who wants to reach the goal. Only one pleasure will finally satisfy the passionate pilgrim: the pleasure of God's company. All tracks lead to the infinitely attractive One. Dispersed energy ruins the whole venture. The pilgrim needs focus to stay on track. The mystics and saints were not sidetracked. They encountered the manifold in the One.

When a person does not drift or coast through one day after another but really lives, deliberately and vigorously, when a person truly *exists*, which literally means to "stand out," when the presence of one singular person makes a significant difference, there is something we are all inclined to say of him or her: "There you have a personality."

An Open Way

Personalities tend to be refreshingly ingenuous, naturally intimate, open and shockingly spontaneous. There is nothing trendy or smarmy about them. They do not loiter or languish listlessly in the foothill of Mt. Carmel (the mythical Mount of Perfection). They wait patiently and prudently enough, but actively and adroitly. Once they detect an open way, they move swiftly and make that way their own, convinced as they are that only along this way can they follow the unique Christ uniquely and unequivocally. For this particular personality, this existential pilgrim, any other way—however popular and pleasant—would be spurious.

Driven by craving, restless egos, most of us do not choose an open way but end up willy-nilly on the wrong path. We are stampeded into marriage, into school, into work. The experience is similar to being forced by relentless traffic off the freeway we have chosen onto an exit we do not want. Incredible trouble!

If we let the Empire or the techno-barbaric juggernaut or the mediocre crowd dictate our path, then the pathologies will proliferate and our sins will unhinge us. We need to plunge courageously into our own open way, not to do our own thing, but to do God's will in our unique way. Deeper levels of life will open up to us as we move with brio and imagination into an ever more real world ruled by Christ.

Christ is unique. Therefore he cannot be copied. Followed yes, copied no. He is the Way, the Truth and the Life—uniquely. We ourselves are commissioned by God to carry our own cross, find our own way, be possessed by all truth and live life fully. We tend to shrink from this privileged burden by imitating the external features of Jesus's life in a shallow and slavish way.

We must climb inside this representative man, immerse ourselves in his mystery, catch his good infection (divinity), put on his mind, enjoying the God-man's wavelength and expanding our constricted hearts to the dimensions of his Sacred Heart. Our religion is so much more a religion *of* Jesus than *about him*. We do not understand the inner state of Jesus or the saints and we try to attain it by the mere mimicry of its outward signs. Nothing good results from that. This kind of un-mystical religion is unproductive drudgery.

The meaning that Christ expressed is God and that is also the meaning of men and women who follow but do not copy him. They act the way they do because they are God-intoxicated people. Their words and deeds, much like the singer and dancer, interpret this experience.

So the path an enlightened pilgrim or personality chooses is one that does not mimic Jesus or the saints and mystics, but one that enables the ordinary secular person to participate as *directly and immediately* as possible in the mystical experience, Christ's own inner experience of his Father and his Father's world—*the real world*, which is the Kingdom of God and not the secular empire. So one pilgrim, for example, Thomas Merton, contemplates, joins the Trappist Order, writes books and becomes a hermit; another, Dorothy Day, prays, writes, and spends the rest of her time and energy in the inner city.

The premise underlying a pilgrim's progress is the cogent hint of a *pathos*[31], a divine reality concerned with the destiny of humanity which mysteriously impinges on history. The supreme issue is whether we are alive or dead to the challenge and expectation of the living God. The crisis engulfs us all. The misery and fear of alienation evokes from all of us a cry of the heart.

---

[31] "Poignancy."

All creatures seem to share this fragility, this angst. At three o'clock this morning between my hermitage and Carmel Lake[32], almost within reach, stood a deer. She lifted her gorgeous head and filled this perfectly still and spectacularly clear night with the deer cry. What a sound! Almost every night this summer I have heard so many riveting voices in these woods—the loon, the owl, the coyote—but deer are notoriously quiet. So this morning when this glorious, gentle beast stood outside my window and cried into my ear, I was beside myself with wonder, right side up with awe. I was bewitched. How astonishing it is to be lifted so dramatically out of the narrow world of human conventions and carried by a sound, at once so earthly and so otherworldly, into a world big and broad, wild and wonderful, and, best of all, unmanageable. For fifteen minutes my mind was engrossed, my heart enlarged; forever after I will know a little more about the inexplicable wildness of God.

By discerning a unique vocation and choosing an open way, true and narrow, the pilgrim finds his or her way into the real world. There is no other way. All other ways are cop-outs. It's ironic how mediocre hordes think that monks and other followers of Christ—the rich variety of lay saints—are the cop-

---

[32] The original article on which this chapter was based was written when McNamara lived at the Nova Scotian hermitage Nova Nada.

outs while the hordes themselves (in truth deluded and enslaved), think they are living in the real world.

Notice in the second paragraph of this chapter the underlined words, "directly and immediately." This is the question we need to ask to determine how alive we are as persons, parishes, and families. How direct and immediate is our participation in the inner life of Christ?

In Pope John Paul II's beautiful letter on *The Consecrated Life*, he reasserts the traditional teaching of the Church: those states of life are higher which are more directly and immediately concerned with God. Every state is conducive to sanctity. But, of course, for all of us, the most direct and immediate relationship with God is the most desirable.

Fecundity and Defection

When Bushmen meet they say "I see you, indeed I see you." To meet, to really meet, to love, to love mindfully, and to act daily in such a way that a permanent, faithful intimacy becomes an eminent possibility—this is the stuff of sanctity.

The common sin is infidelity, due to weariness of spirit. The common grace is transformation of matter by spirit. Being partners with God in that transformation is the most exciting thing in the world. As G. K. Chesterton said, "We can make something beautiful by loving it in all its ugliness." Our progressively easy ways out of life and love—or out of the "dark nights[33]" that lead to undreamt of levels of life and love—are not pilgrim ways. Divorce, abortion, euthanasia, and defection clutter the way with disasters. Let the Empire legislate in favor of caducity and rapacity. The Kingdom thrives on liberty, the freedom to plod and plod right merrily on the sacred earth, fed by the delight of creatures and led by the light of Spirit, until a way opens; then plunge single-mindedly and wholeheartedly into the fire of Love.

One of the words I just used to signify human perfidy needs, once clarified, to be used again unmincingly in our public vocabulary. The word is "defection." Fecund means to bond and germinate, to be fruitful. I can preach and teach all I want. If I do not bond, there is no fruit. Another noticeable thing: where original bonds wither so does the fruit. There are manifold defections—from professions of faith; from marital, religious, and priestly vows; from private and public commitments; from pledges of allegiance to a land, a cause, a friendship. We have idiotically become accustomed to defections, but they are nonetheless the most perfidious

---

[33] Here, McNamara is referring to the "dark night of the soul"—a condition where one has no real reassurance or felt presence of God (see writings by St. John of the Cross). Saint Theresa of Calcutta's dark night is perhaps the most commonly known modern example. There is no shortcut out of a "dark night" despite our current culture's promises.

of human calamities. More than anything else, they account for our fractured society, our cultural decay.[34]

Through prizing silence and solitude, pilgrims do not venture forth in isolation. Their contemplation is not private and precious. It is personal and perilous. In this complex and meretricious world, seeing and telling things as they really are is imperative. In fact, real contemplatives have the deepest and most far-reaching effect on the sociopolitical world. As the salt of the earth, they prevent this world from going bad. They are the leaven of the new creation. As such, they must remain in the lump—aware of it and loving it no matter how solitary they themselves remain. Their involvement in "this world," to be the soul in what Saint Paul calls "this body of death" (Romans 7:24), means sharing not only in the sovereignty, but in the suffering and the endurance which are ours in Jesus (Revelations 1:9). Contemplatives are "kept in this world as in a prison house…yet they themselves hold the world together….So great is the office for which God has appointed them and which *is not lawful for them to decline*" (Saint Paul).

Contemplative pilgrims—unstuck humans—rescue the Church from its prevalent weakness by supplying prophecy in the true biblical sense. The

---

[34] McNamara adds this aside: On the other hand, I could write a book on the holiness of divorced people and laicized priests and religious who continued to follow Christ.

Church speaks with irresistible authority when its voice is both theological *and* political. Moralizing is a cheap substitute. The humanization of human beings depends on honest confrontation. Pious palaver from "professional" priests and ecclesiastical apparatchiks is not what the world needs in its pulpits. To speak smooth words, to reassure, to utter inanities to a desperate people is an act of cruelty and contempt. If religious leaders are pilgrims themselves, rooted but plainly en route through the ambiguities and vicissitudes of this age, their chief occupation will be to evoke trust—a deep faith—and lead us all through the portals of the "dark night." Only when pilgrims get the bad news, the way things really are, will they listen attentively to the good news. Conflict and suffering, darkness and dereliction, when grasped with an eternal perspective, will provide for pilgrims the best conditions for enlightenment.

The pilgrim's puzzle is the following: how does one take God with ultimate seriousness, and at the same time undertake the journey with scrumptious, impetuous glee? To sustain the meaning of this basic paradox we need keen guidance. People like Paul Tillich and Alan Watts raised the question but botched the guidance.

Holy Worldliness

Saint Paul is a superb journeyman and guide. First of all, he affirms this world and this life: "If in this life only we have hoped in Christ we are all of men most to be pitied" (1 Corinthians 15:19). To identify with the world alienated from God, the Empire, is sheer folly. To be immersed in the real world, in the kingdom of God, under the Messianic reign of Christ, is to be holy. The contrast Paul makes is not between life before death and life after. What he is contrasting with hope in this life only is not life beyond the grave, but life in Christ, in union with God, here and now. He does not deny that life beyond the grave is an essential part of the Christian Testament. He simply emphasizes the pilgrimage we freely begin and finish on earth. The whole journey unfolds in the resurrected order of being—in this world, and in large measure, for it.

The important distinction is between this age and the age to come, both before death. The Greeks made a spatial distinction, but the Hebrews' distinction is temporal. My own interpretation of "this age" is life before the "dark night" and "the age to come" is life after the "dark night." The Passover is from "the sufferings of the present time to the glory that is to be revealed" (Romans 8:18). In the Bible, earth is not to be scrapped in favor of heaven or left behind in order to go there. The promise is "a new heaven and a new earth" (2 Peter 3:13). The word for "new" is *kairos* rather than *neos*, which means renewal here and now, rather than a fresh start at a new site. Jesus's call is not to otherworldliness but to holy worldliness.

So in responding wholly to the summons of Being in its manifold evocations, pilgrims repudiate the Empire, not the world. Perceived demands of love alone claim the pilgrim's loyalty. Many religions say, "Do not love the world." The Christian religion says, "He so loved the world..." (John 3:16). As God-lovers we may not lose our hearts to the world but are asked to give our lives for the world. That is why I always think of a Solemn Profession as a religious commitment with incalculable political ramifications. Why consecrate oneself? The answer is in Saint Paul's letter to the Philippians: "that your politics may be worthy of the Gospel of Christ" (Philippians 1:27). The Greek word Paul uses is *politeuesthe*.

The Church is no longer a threat to the State; no need to worry about separation. The problem now is the complicity of the Church in the culture of oppression and of mammon. The Church is a pilgrim people. To fulfill its mission, the Church must become more detached and more involved. Pilgrims are not called to be servants of the state, but rather its conscience and a witness that it stand under judgment. This is not a proclamation reserved for bishops and universities; it is the prophetic vocation of the man on the street and the monk in the wilderness. What we all need to do is listen to the Word, absorb and assimilate it. We should "eat the scroll" (Ezekiel 3:1). Then, eschewing all fatuous inanities, and all words that are violent, vulgar, and obscene, we should tell the awful but irrepressible truth.

God called himself the One who is always there ("I am who am"). We co-create with him by being there.[35] Presence is what makes a person lovely and lively. Just as personality refers to a person who is really there, spirituality means something like that: the human spirit meeting the challenge of everyday life with such discreet vigor that a perceptible style ensues, a style redolent of Christ—not a wooden imitation but a creative embodiment of the same Holy Spirit enfleshed peerlessly and incandescently in Jesus.

The Founder of Christianity expects his followers to "do even greater things than he" (John 14:12), and endowed by the same Spirit they can and sometimes do. The lives of the saints are vivid portrayals of how the Spirit that blazed divinely in Christ continues to inflame his ardent followers. The pilgrim lets nothing impede either the fundamental awareness of the Ineffable or the total immersion of the whole self in the concrete contextual situation of historical existence.

I am commanded therefore I am. If addressed here, I am wholly here; if there, I am wholly there. In the words of Isaiah: "Here I am, Lord, send me" (1 Samuel 1:16). "Here I am" is the life-stance of the pilgrim. Being there, presence, is the heart of the journey.

---

[35] McNamara notes "He was not there for me" is the victim's trivialization of this profound truth.

The acclamations, explanations, descriptions and evaluations come later and depend on presence recalled. The mystic, pilgrim par excellence, is an ordinary person extraordinarily present to another human existence, to the exigencies of everyday and to the Holy One who suffuses all things with meaning and love.

The mysticism of the prophets is both frightening and refreshing. No solemn solipsism here. The naked Word of God is heard and the prophet is hurled into enemy camps, slums, palaces and caves. This God-filled person is where God wants to be and says without flinching what the Absolute requires of us.

At the end of the road, in the opening way to transcendence, where everydayness is breached and simplicity is reached, there is genuine mystical experience: the presence of God felt. Only here in the cognitive depths do humans become, indeed, in fact, the image and likeness of God.

The steadfast pilgrim, keeping steady pace along the way and spurred on by the fascinating freshness of things, beckoned by grace under pressure of things met, moves deftly and deliberately toward the One who not only refreshes but ravishes and rewards such passionate pitch with full life and lavish feast. It is a feast of love: alterity—meeting God, not separately, not apart, but at the heart of the world, the underground of being. All ever met *en route* are met here *au courant*.

The pilgrim's purpose is more life, more love. Living is loving and loving is dying. Here I am; send me, spend me, use me up—for the others. So Christ, that manliest man, that purest pilgrim, sensed everything, enjoyed everything while he set his face toward Jerusalem, toward death. On Tabor Jesus insists "Do not tell of this glory until I suffer" (Mark 9:9).

Being shaped by the pleasure and pain of living, responding sincerely to all the surprises of his Father's will, was Christ's spirituality. In view of this all our modern techniques for consciousness raiding, for self-realization, seem embarrassingly banal. Ultimately the human pilgrimage is the way of the cross. Fidelity to the cross—the devastating demands of love—issues in the resurgence of life, in Resurrection. To be human is to be a lover. To endure is to resurrect. All the creatures the lover once met, and is bound to leave on *that* level, share the same cry of anguished ardor: "Where goest Thou, my love?" And the beloved, faithful to each and all, share this response: "To Skull Hill to be crucified for you."

Chapter Three

The Call—Erotic[36] Holiness

The Call

*I*t takes many forms and shapes—often calamitous, serendipitous, terpsichorean, threatening and seductive. The diaphanous universe is God's megaphone. Revelation is not the incursion of the supernatural but openness to the wonder of everyday—the enormous lights and miracles with which the world is filled. A naturalist points out to the Founder of the Hasidim, the Ball Shem Tov, that God's people who escaped from Egypt crossed the Red Sea because of the natural unfolding of the scientific nature

---

[36] In an unpublished essay entitled "Wanted: Monastic Giants in a Shrunken Age," McNamara defines "Eros" as the "Absolute (Divine) proposal (that) requires an absolute response. This, in turn, requires bravery and courage. This is no vocation for a sissy, a softy or a sophist."

of things[37]. The sea would have parted at that time and place regardless of the plight of Israel. The Ball Shem Tov's reply: "Is it not a miracle enough that the people should arrive at the Red Sea exactly at that time and place?"

One reason why there are so few vocations today is that the whole passionate, romantic, erotic and apostolic thing is in most minds tied up with an external, official call from a bishop, abbot, religious superior, or the boss. The true vocational source—spousal intimacy with God—has been lost. Once we came out of the deeps and settled for a shallow, superficial existence, vocations withered. The institutional factor is necessary but secondary. Listening and discerning require one to be still at the center. It is good to have a strong protective carapace, but the center of life cannot be the carapace. If the life withers within, if contemplation—a long, loving look at the real—fades, it cannot be revived by the carapace. The inner call is when our direct relationship with Christ himself is in question and that must be the heart of all vocations. This address and coquetry at the apex of our being is

---

[37] In 2017, Tampa, Florida experienced a highly unusual 6-foot drop in sea levels that exposed the bottom of Tampa Bay for over 100 yards. The phenomenon was related to Hurricane Irma (not a tsunami, which is the usual cause for such things). But even given this, I agree with the Ball Shem Tov—for the Israelis to be at the Red Sea at the right time was miracle enough.

the prompting of the Holy Spirit and often happens in a flash. Note what von Balthasar [38] says:

> Even now after thirty years, I could still go to that remote path in the Black Forest, not far from the Basel, and find again the tree beneath which I was struck as by lightning….And yet it was neither theology nor the priesthood which then came into my mind in a flash. It was simply this: you have nothing to choose, you have been called. You will not serve; you will be taken into service. You have no plans to make; you are just a little stone in a mosaic which has long been ready. All I needed to do was "leave everything and follow" without making plans, without wishes or insights. All I needed to do was to stand there and wait and see what I would be needed for. (*Hans Urs von Balthasar*, ed. David Schindler, pg 11)

Cardinal John Henry Newman wrote about the intimacy, ecstasy, and fecundity of the early Church. Prayer produced and sustained vocations. The early Church was shaped by the people under the inspired

---

[38] Hans Urs von Balthasar 1905 – 1988.

leadership of a few great men. One of these was Evagrius of Pontus. He is the one who defined a theologian as one whose prayer is True. We could define a Christian the same way. The following story tells us what happens when our prayer is untrue:

> An atheist was walking through the woods admiring all the so-called "accidents of evolution." "What majestic trees! What powerful rivers! What beautiful animals!" he said to himself. As he was walking alongside the river he heard a rustling in the bushes behind him. He turned to look. He saw a seven-foot grizzly charge toward him. He ran as fast as he could up the path. He looked over his shoulder and saw that the bear was closing in. He ran even faster, so scared that tears were coming to his eyes. He looked over his shoulder again, and the bear was even closer. His heart was pumping frantically and he tried to run even faster. He tripped and fell on the ground. He rolled over to pick himself up but saw the bear right on top of him, reaching for him with his left paw and raising his right paw to strike. At that instant the atheist cried out, "Oh my God!" Time stopped. The bear froze. The forest was silent. Even

the river stopped moving. As a bright light shone upon the man, a voice came out of the sky. "You deny My existence for all these years, teach others I don't exist, and even credit creation to a cosmic accident. Do you expect Me to help you out of this predicament? Am I to count you as a believer?" The atheist looked directly into the light. "It would be hypocritical to ask to be a Christian after all these years, but perhaps you could make the bear a Christian?" "Very well," said the Voice. The light went out. The river ran again. The sounds of the forest resumed. And then the bear dropped his right paw...brought both paws together...bowed his head and spoke. "Lord, for this food which I am about to receive, I am truly thankful."

Prayer inspires one who is called and enables her to listen, to follow, to be an adept; that is, one who moves daringly into deeper levels of being and sets the stage in society for paradigmatic shifts. One who becomes a seer, who returns from the perilous journey and shares with all an undreamt of experience of fire, of divine union.

Now, the Revolution. Because all revolutions are tainted and many corrupt, shall we refrain from calling ourselves and becoming ourselves revolutionaries by our Christian-ness? Israel, to the Hebrew Bible, means the actual people Israel who became a people through the Sinai Covenant and who remain one insofar as they are faithful to this covenant. This covenant, as we know, is to become "a kingdom of priests and a holy people." A "holy people" does not mean to become a collection of well-meaning individuals, but a true community that acts as such: imitating God's justice, right-eousness, and holiness in the human adventure and in the social, political, economic, and international life of the people. There is no distinction here between the religious and social since the religious for biblical man is not a separate dimension transcending history, but instead the demand that the transcendent places on us in history.

Jesus does not take our place in redeeming the world but enables us to fulfill the task with him. The nature of Jesus's vocation is captured to some degree in various scriptural passages, but most of all, I think, during the forty days of wrestling with Satan in the wilderness where we see the temptations of a man who knows himself called and yet must discover again in each new situation just what it means that he is called. In the case of Joan of Arc and Thomas Becket a shining category—martyrdom—awaited them with glory. Jesus, however, had to go through the terrible tension of a unique call and work it out as he responded, with his whole being in utter anguish and heroic trust, to the demand of the historical moment.

The vocational climax is reached on Calvary, unprecedented and unrepeated in the long turbulent centuries of human life, when the Son of Man prays on the Cross, "Eli, Eli, lama sabachtani." He is not merely reciting a psalm as those given to an exaggerated theism suppose; he is rather experiencing again the raw anguish of the unique vocation in which he has answered the call but in this crucial moment feels nothing and fears everything.

Oh sweet and terrible mystery of life! I love your mystery, Lord, more than all our clever solutions. I could never live without your wrath. It is, after all, your infinite care and concern, your Eros, that lies behind it all. Even historical histrionics seem inevitable, if only we endure the dialogue and cling tenaciously to the covenant. Seeking our presence, you ask again and again, "Where art thou?" Your longing for our presence, your demanding an account is your "mercy."

Failure doesn't matter; fidelity does. There's a joyful agony if we suffer for his sake. As Pascal said, "Christ is in agony until the end of the world; we must not rest in the meantime." We need not know why we suffer as long as we suffer for his sake.

Every human situation calls us out. We become identified and integrated insofar as we gather together

all the possibilities of the self into a caring, loving response. In the act itself the integration of the person
occurs. A principle governs this endeavor; namely, action is often father and mother of a longed-for disposition, a required virtue, or a desirable accomplish-
ment. For instance, I was extremely shy of public
speaking and writing for publication. Strongly urged
to do it by my superiors, I did, and have been doing it
ever since, and sometimes with felicity. Since ultimately it is Life that calls forth our character, all we
must do is immerse ourselves in life.

My favorite image of that is the dog who goes
into the ocean, comes out, and with utmost vigor
shakes off every drop of water—then once again
plunges into the sea. An opposite image conveys the
same madcap spirit: fish, irrepressible, jumping out of
the water, drinking in wild, wondrous air that would
kill any ordinary fish. Those fish really live! Finally,
how often we've all discovered how in rescuing an
ugly situation, or a paltry, even a disreputable person,
we become whole ourselves!

When we connect with or attend to what is not ourselves, we bring ourselves into wholeness from the
depths of our being in response to this call. What we call
our evil urge should be dedicated to the service of God.
The evil urge is transformed as it helps energize the soul;
the soul which is focused and eminently disposed for the
kiss of the Spouse, for divine union. This requires all of

us to turn radically and ruthlessly away from tedium and trivia toward ultimate communion.

A story: The Rabbi of Rizhyn laid the fingers of his right hand on the table after the morning meal and said: "God says to Israel: 'Return unto me…and I will return unto you.'" Then he turned his right hand palm up and said: "But we children of Israel reply, 'Turn Thou us unto Thee, O Lord and we shall be turned; renew our days as of old.' For our exile is heavy on us and we have not the strength to return to you of ourselves." And then he turned his palm down again and said: "But the Holy One, blessed be He, says: 'First you must return unto me.'" Four times the Rabbi of Rizhyn turned his hand, palm up and palm down. But in the end he said: "The children of Israel are right, though, because it is true that the waves of anguish close over them and they cannot govern their hearts and turn to God.'"

This story from the Hasidim illustrates true prayer: an authentic dialogue about a living situation. Do we have enough gumption to turn at *this* time, in *this* exile? To God, the rabbi says "Let's talk." This tale, emphasizing our ongoing personal relationship with the Underground of our being, the Holy Ineffable Presence, relates us simultaneously and existentially to the shocking and shattering contingencies of the day. That is where we pray, thus riding with exhilaration the waves of anxiety—sometimes in doubt, acting as if it is the call. It usually is! At other times, it means listening to the person standing in front of you: "I see you," "I love you," "I wed you." This opens you to experience the background call of the universe.

Life itself is calling. Who, though, will dare live life? We seem more intent upon buffers rather than boosters of life. "Hooters," for instance, are buffers. The television anesthetizes by its buff presentations. The events, whether garish or ghoulish, are dependably simulacra pseudo-events. That is why encounters with reality are rare and always overwhelming.

What is pressingly important is for us to be acutely ready for a summons of any caliber. The evocation of the universal call prepares us for the quotidian summons. We, as living witnesses, need to be ambulatory answers to the call, moving steadfastly toward more freedom, and, ultimately, divine union.

A scholar approached Abba Bunam: "Why does God inspire the enslaved Jews by accentuating the First Commandment when the Creation story is far more impressive?" Abba Bunam's reply: "Heaven and earth! That's sublime. They would very piously dismiss it. So God said 'I am the one who fished you out of the mud. So come right over here and listen to me.'"

The Word is enough truth for all and forever. We need to hear the pure, raw expression of sheer Eros; we need to be smitten by hitherto unheard of Beauty ("No one ever spoke like this man"); we need to taste and test his worldwide, uncompromising revolution.

We need to abandon our own flatulent fluvial of words, words, words as we are shaken and then shaped by what Saint John of the Cross refers to as the One Word spoken from all eternity and reaching its culminating apotheosis in Christ, ever ancient, ever new, so that nothing remains to be said. Let us rivet on him and be transformed.

We need desperately to learn to listen, a discipline foreign to most people everywhere. Recent technological devices—the mobile phone, for instance—have heightened the clamor and the chaos and reduced the possibility to change, to cultivate wisdom which is a taste for the right things. Here is a simple wisdom test, in fact a human test: What things are more likely to relate you more directly and immediately to the Living God? Choose no more than five things, reject everything else. One hint: you will get nowhere without silence and solitude.

Let me tell you about Tommy Sully: Father Murphy was eager to get in touch with Dr. Henry Sully, so he phoned him at home. His son, Tommy, about ten years old, answered the phone. "Tommy, is your dad there?" "Yes, but he's very busy." "Your mom home?" "She's busy as well." "Anyone else?" "Uncle Pat, but he's cranky and busy, Father. You don't want him." "Well, anyone else then?" "Yes, the police." "Oh my, put one on." "I can't Father. They are so busy it's scary." "All right Tommy. I'm a fool, but I'm asking one more time. Anyone else?" "Yes, the fire-men." "Yeah, yeah, I know, Tommy. They are all frightfully busy. Tell me one thing: what the heck are they all doing?" "Father, they are looking for me!"[39]

Even young people seek solitude to be alone with God and therefore are one with him.

That happens to you and me all the time. People are always looking for us. But so is the Hound of Heaven[40], the Lion of Judah, the Word of God. As Saint Paul says, we belong to him. He calls incessantly because we belong to him. Alienated, we are misera-ble, unnatural. In communion, in conversation, we are wisely and wittily onto something. We are uproari-ously happy.

He came to set our hearts on fire. He wants us flaming now. The whole strategy of love commenced as soon as the fishermen found him. "Where do you live, Stranger?" Come and see. They learned from him first hand, and they were goners. They became wild men—disciplined wild men in love with God and his whole creation. They became Zorbatic long before Zorba: "Everyone needs a little bit of madness; other-wise he will never cut the rope and be free."

---

[39] McNamara makes this note: Looking for Tommy is looking for Christ.
[40] Francis Thompson's (1859 – 1907) "Hound of Heaven" was first published in 1893, but is more readily available in *The Divine Office. Christian Prayer: The Liturgy of the Hours*. Catholic Book Publishing Co. NY. 1976.

The holy hound's question was: "What think ye of Christ?" How come? Well, "he who sees me sees the Father." Now there are three contemporary authors of Christian-ness who speak with passionate and pellucid clarity: One, J.D. Salinger says, "See Christ and you are a Christian. All else is talk." Secondly, the author Francois Mauriac writes, "Once you get to know him you cannot be cured of him…Oh how avidly people would listen to you if you spoke to them no longer as sociologists, psychologist, theologians and experts on modern trivia but as men and women who have seen and touched the Resurrected Christ."

Finally, "Sharon's Christmas Prayer," by John Shea[41]:

> She was five,
> sure of the facts,
> and recited them
> with slow solemnity
> convinced every word
> was a revelation.
>
> She said
>
> they were so poor

---

[41] John Shea, *The Hour of the Unexpected*, Allan, Texas, Argus Communications, 1977.

they had only peanut butter and jelly sand-
wiches
to eat
and they went a long way from home
without getting lost. The lady rode
a donkey, the man walked, and the baby
was inside the lady.
They had to stay in a stable
with an ox and ass (hee-hee)
but the Three Rich Men
found them because a star lited the roof.
Shepherds came and you could
pet the sheep but not feed them.
Then the baby was borned.
And do you know who he was?

Her quarter eyes inflated
to silver dollars.

The baby was God.

And she jumped in the air
whirled around, dove into the sofa
and buried her head under the cushion,
which is the only proper response
to the Good News of the Incarnation.

Chapter Four

The Desert Experience

*T*he Desert is fundamental; its sands run through all salvation history and the whole tradition of the Church. The trek through the desert was a liberation for the Israelites. Full of promise, of hope, of life, it was still a road of suffering and trial.

The Desert is always a challenge, an invitation to a contest. The contest here is whether or not we can come to terms with the bare and undiminished facts of reality—the reality of our deluded and denatured self and that self's devastated and dehumanized world, and the reality of God.

We cannot live a good human life without silence and solitude. The Desert offers these but they are merely conditions for what the desert meant more fundamentally to the people of the Bible: a place of trial and struggle, a proving ground; a place where the values of life are presented in clear, stark terms; a place where either you take the initiative, in a wise and knowing way, in favor of living, or the forces of nature get the better of you.

We need this confrontation with the wild, untamed forces of nature. We have trifled too long in the genteel tradition. We have not dug deeply enough. We have slipped too easily into a spinster-ish concern for the pretty instead of the beautiful. We have come to think of the natural world as a condition instead of a great force, and are content to experience it only superficially—a far cry from Maurice Blondel's[42] description of life as the "experience of the inexhaustible."

In *Walden*, Hendry David Thoreau expounds that immersion in nature is essential to the human spirit and why that is so: "We can never have enough of nature. We must be refreshed by the sea coast with its wrecks, the sight of the inexhaustible vigor, vast and titanic features, the wilderness with its living and decayed trees, the thundercloud, and the rain which lasts three weeks and produces freshets. We need to witness our own limits transgressed, and some life pasturing freely where we never wander...I love to see that nature is so rife with life that myriads can be afforded to be sacrificed and suffered to prey on one another; that tender organisms can be so serenely

---

[42] Blondel (1861-1949), a French philosopher, was best known for his work, "Action."

squashed out of existence like pulp—tadpoles which herons gobble up, and tortoises and toads run over in the road; and that sometimes it has rained flesh and blood!...Poison is not poisonous after all, nor are our wounds fatal."

Powerful as our weapons are, vast as is the destruction we are capable of, there is something still more powerful than we. That something is in part the least amicable but also the most enduring aspect of what Thoreau called "wildness," and it may survive when we have destroyed the better order we tried to make. By managing nature we may to some extent discipline it. We may also, in the process of becoming human, shift somewhat the emphases in its complex of impulses and powers. But we cannot dispense with the wildness without becoming near-machines and therefore less, not more, than the animal we tried to transcend. And so our man-centered humanism backfires and dehumanizes us.

The desert is a place where an egotistic and complacent humanism will not go. It will undo you. Jesus was led into the desert, we remember, to be tried by the devil. The early spiritual fathers in the Church—who we called the Desert Fathers—went out into the desert just to come to terms with Satan, with the forces of evil. Each human being, being another Christ, must come to terms actively with the evil forces within themselves. The word of God calls us to take the initiative against the forces within us. And we must take the initiative. For Original Sin is not just an isolated difficulty or an occasional failure. Original Sin means that our whole life was once organized for disaster, for destruction, for death. We must take the initiative in reforming, in reconstructing our life in Christ. This is what God has in mind for us when he calls us into the desert. This is the wisdom of the desert. This is its meaning.

The Desert evokes the human, latent capacity for initiative, exploration, evaluation. It interrupts our ordinary pattern of life. It intercepts the stultifying process of a conventional, routine piety. It disengages us from the regular round of respectable human activities. We learned to be still, alert, perceptive, recollective, so that issues become clear, reality becomes recognizable and unambiguous. We see real things, not just shadows; experience events, not just continued pseudo-events. We know ourselves, not just a projected or statistically palled image of ourselves. We know God. Not abstractions about God, not even the theology of God, but the much more mysterious and mighty God of theology—the God of Abraham; of Moses; of Elijah; of Peter, Paul, and John; of the Fathers and Mothers of the Desert; the God of Saints and the God of sinners.

Desert spirituality means much more than just getting out of the "rat race." Even the human Christ needed periods of solitary prayer, times set apart. Deep down in every person is the ineluctable need to recognize and proclaim God's absolute sovereignty. We have a need, however hidden, to turn completely to God, a need for a kind of suspension of our horizontal relation with other creatures[43]. And if we manage to go through life without this need ever rising above the threshold of consciousness, it simply proves how gutted and distorted our humanity is, how completely befuddled our sense of values is. Even as natural men and women we are not living to the full extent of our human nature until we respond to the periodic need to turn from our passing human activities to stand before God and belong exclusively to him. What then, should be our experienced need as a child of God but to turn habitually with loving trust to the Father and forget everything but him and his care for us? This, too, is the prudence of the desert, wisdom in action.

But even this bearing witness to the totality of the claim that God and the things of God have upon us is not the deepest meaning of the desert tradition of spirituality. There is one essential thing about the desert:

---

[43] McNamara once told me the pattern on the cross is both horizontal "de humanis" and vertical "de Divinis," reaching out to humanity and reaching up to God.

it is the place where we encounter God. It is the place where God comes out to meet us. It is the place where God visits his people. This is why the tradition of the desert spirituality has persisted in the Church. The words God spoke through Hosea are always significant: "I shall espouse you in faith, lead you into the desert and speak to your heart."

The time in the desert for the Israelites was a special time of miracles. There was no other time of wonders like it in all the Old Testament. A time of miraculous healing, food from heaven, water rushing forth from the desert rocks, God guiding his people with cloud and fire. We left Egypt under his protection. His strong arm was with us; he led the way, his hand was held out to us. The road through the desert was literally sprinkled with the wonderful deeds of God, his saving events. The glorious deeds we pray about in the Psalms almost always echo back to the desert years. At no time was God more tenderly caring for his people than in the desert.

This desert tradition in spirituality is a long one, stretching back into the Old Testament, and it is a wide one, spreading beyond the Christian tradition to wherever men and women seek God. Because of this it necessarily is still with us today—in the world, in the Church, and in every individual's life. God's loving care still goes before us, leading us with the pillar of fire by night that signifies the fire of love, and with the cloud by day that guides us by the obscure light of faith. He tenderly feeds all the hungers of the human heart, the greatest of these being our hunger for God. This he feeds with nothing less than bread that is his own body, food that makes us one with him. Like Elijah, who ran for his life into the desert to escape from Jezebel, we too must wake up from our stupor and eat of the hearth cake the angel has brought us so as to have strength for the journey to the mountain of God. ("...Arise, eat, because the journey is too great for you." 1 Kings 19:5-7.) Jesus himself is the True Bread that comes down from heaven, and he himself assures us that unless we eat of that Bread we will not have life in us. Our desert journey has brought us now to the central mystery of the enfleshment of God in his creation: the mystery of the Eucharist.

If we are ever to cross over this Desert without delay or anxiety, if we are ever going to enjoy the "Passover," then our sole contentment as wayfarers and pilgrims of the Absolute must be divine; that is to say, we must be God-centered human beings, earthly enfleshments of the Numinous. Western mysticism is necessarily earthy. The source of Christian mysticism is in the earth, the world, the flesh. This does not mean confinement but contentment. God has revealed that he is content to dwell in us and finds delight in us when we embody him. And when we enflesh him consciously and *creatively*, there is no end to his delight. It is as unconfined as an active volcano. In a second sense, there is divine contentment in the human venture.

God in the flesh means God in the heart. Prayer is a cry of the heart. Whose prayer do we hear in the Hallelujah Chorus and the wailing at the Wall, and the laughter of children, the scream from the bed and the howl from the Cross? At the heart of hearts is the cry. It is the source of all music and all gladness, all joy and all sadness. To learn to be in tune with that cry and then to intone it with all our heart and all our breath—this is what it means to live. The cry that summons us into being, into life, into undreamed of realms of love, is the eternal, infinite reality that the New Testament refers to as "the Word." Saint John says, "In the beginning was the Word…And the Word was made flesh" (John: 1, 14). The Word was made flesh originally, not in the age of Caesar Augustus, but in the beginning. The Incarnation did not begin with Christmas but with creation. The Incarnation reached its peak in Jesus, who expresses the Word, verbally and bodily, with such a degree of amplitude that no Christology has been able to fit "this man" into our mental categories.

The flesh that God became in the beginning was raw matter, the stuff of the universe. It is highly significant that the tradition has always associated the Word or the Logos with the original act of creation, the act of God that goes on and on. At the heart of everything is the supreme initiative of the One who acts, the One who is always there. At work and at leisure, God is there. On each of the six days of creation, he is there. And on the seventh day, God is there. History is the story of how humans became co-creators. And we will continue to be co-creators, builders of the Kingdom, until the One who in the beginning chose to dwell in us will come again, reassert his sovereign claim, and gather all our fragmented and estranged shreds of being into the reconciled opposites of the one Word. As Saint John of the Cross said, from all eternity God speaks one word: nothing remains to be said.

The Word resounds in us because God does not act in a vacuum. We bring to the cry of God a little fulfillment. And to the degree that we do so, we bring on the Parousia[44]. As the Word resonates in us, the mystery of faith unfolds, the enfleshment of God increases. This enfleshment provides for us a focus of what would otherwise be invisible and unbearable. Such incredible becomings: the divine becoming human, the infinite becoming finite, the spiritual becoming material, and the eternal becoming subject to time and space. The Word reaches its finest focus in Jesus. It will reach its final expression in the Parousia. We live between the focus and the fulfillment. It is

---

[44] The Second Coming. See Matthew 24-25.

by coping creatively with the exigencies of life that we engage in the perpetual and progressive enfleshment of God. The Creator has entrusted himself to creation, to our freedom. He is always there; pure Spirit, longing to be enfleshed.

God requires our trustful cooperation through creative activity. The Kingdom has been handed over to us. We are entrusted with God and his world, with the totality of being. God and humanity are involved mutually in self-actualizing surrender. We trust the One who trusts us with the future of the planet and the well-being of our neighbor. If we replace this grateful allegiance to God with a fearful, tight grip on our own homemade egos, the activities of life take a destructive turn. Our interpersonal and international relationships become chaotic because we are so unrelated to that which is the ultimate real: God in us, the Word made flesh. There is no human peace without divine communion.

In order to engage in truly creative activity, we must learn to unite contemplation and action. Action without contemplation is blind. When we are driven into feverish activity that is not inspired and empowered by contemplation we do more harm than good. Our busyness enslaves us. Those who succeed us then will be even busier and more encumbered. They will be forced to undo all that we have done because our work was not inspired by the Holy Spirit and therefore did not prepare the way for a progressive enfleshment of the Logos.

So for action to be meaningful, there must also be stillness. *Stillness* characterizes that harmonious activity of human beings we call creative activity—the stillness of an artist at work, the stillness of a dancer ready to leap. The stillness of creative activity is very different from a flaccid, limp kind of relaxation. At the ending of Morning Prayer in a small community dear to my heart we pray this Shaker prayer: "Now is the time to be still. And we will." In the evening a relaxed kind of stillness and quietude is enjoyed, but mornings are characterized by a creative, forceful, unpredictable kind of stillness that leads, we hope, through active contemplation into creative activity. If God so pleases, we are then led beyond creative activity into passive contemplation. But we must first be responsible ourselves for an active kind of contemplation that leads desirably into creative activity, because creative activity is the realm of the enfleshed Logos.

Only a free person is capable of creative activity and so, ultimately, capable of God. Freedom does not mean doing anything we want to do. It means really wanting to do what we must to open up all the taut teguments of the flesh to the power of the Spirit. Jesus was so utterly free and thus so thoroughly imbued with divine love that he became Christ. In this definitive denouement of the Word made flesh, God reconciled all things to himself. The Church, the body of Christ, continues this reconciliation by prolonging and extending the enfleshment of the Word into the farthest reaches of the world.

In the Church the Eucharist plays a central role. Every Eucharist remembers Jesus. Understand that the word "remembers" is precisely the opposite of "dismembers." At every Eucharist the body of Christ takes a visible shape. During the priestly Memorial action of the Church, because of the presence and power of its head, bread and wine, pieces of cosmic material bearing the marks of human industry and creative activity, become capable of mediating to people the vitality of Christ in a particularly powerful way. The consecrated bread and wine focus with special sharpness the wider reality I'm trying to highlight: the enfleshment of God in all flesh. The Eucharist is a celebration of this marvelous mystery as well as a focused embodiment of it. This enfleshment means that the Word is as much a part of the universe as a hydrogen atom. Like Christ and the Church, the Eucharist is a focus of the enfleshed Word. It is not a closed event but open-ended and outward looking. The intrinsic dynamism of the Eucharist extends infinitely beyond the boundaries of the liturgical actions of the Church. We must recognize this link between liturgy and life, between worship and work. Otherwise we become stultified and disgrace the universal Church.

There are three dramatic and practical implications of the enfleshed Logos. <u>First</u>, *there is no such thing as divine intervention.* How can a transcendent God who is simultaneously imminent, who is already operating through the Logos from within the entire universe, come from or act from without? Ordinarily the Incarnation is designated as the finest example of intervention. Not so. The Incarnation is simply the supreme focus. <u>Another implication</u> of the enfleshed Logos is that *there is no separation between the transcendent God and the material world; there is no careful demarcation between the sacred and the secular.* We still need specially sacred places and specially sacred times. But there is no dichotomy between the sacred and the profane.

<u>Finally</u>, if the enfleshment of the Logos is perpetual, progressive, and universal, *the spiritual is not necessarily superior to the material. The material is spiritual.*

But we must acknowledge that there is human activity that is destructive and therefore not possibly within the realm of the enfleshed Logos. This destructive human activity opposes the creative activity of the enfleshed Logos and is called evil. As we take a strong stand against evil, we push back the barriers and extend the domain of the enfleshed Logos.

The enfleshed Logos has a fourfold focus: Christ, the Church, the Eucharist, and the Consecration. The Eucharist is the event where the faithful gather together and provide a visible, tangible, palpable exam-ple and embodiment of the Church, and the Conse-cration comprises the central dominical words and ac-tions of the liturgy by which the bread and wine be-come the body and blood of Christ. So, you have the Incarnate Word containing Christ, Christ containing the Church, the Church containing the Eucharist, and the Eucharist containing the Consecration. It is im-portant to note that this order cannot be reversed: Christ does not contain or confine the enfleshed Word of God, the Church does not contain or confine Christ, the Eucharist does not contain or constrict the Church, and the Consecration itself is so dynamic that it bursts the boundaries of the Eucharistic celebration, touching and uplifting the whole world.

Only now do I dare say something about Christ-mas. What does Christmas teach us? The mystery of Christmas claims that in that Baby and the Man who grew from him, we find the clue to the meaning of all life. The Christmas Gospel, the "Good News" of Christmas, the "tidings of great joy," reveal that what we see in Jesus teaches us more about the heart of the universe than anything else.

Regardless of what we see on the surface of life, however absurd, shallow, or mundane, we discover at the bottom of it all what Christ looks like, sounds like, is. So it is important to get to the bottom of the mystery of all mysteries, to the bottom of the universe, to the rock bottom that is love upon which the whole universe is constructed.

The naked truth of Christ enthralled the writers of the New Testament. They wanted to convey the ultimate significance of Christ, who was so astonishing, so absolutely unselfish, that we could see right through him as through a window into the Godhead. God was in Christ! Christ was in fact the God-man! This is the central proclamation of the New Testament writers. Because they were men of their age, a supernaturalist age, they indicated this divinity of Christ in the only way they knew how: with a glint of glory, a flutter of wings, and a display of sheer miracle.

But today, the poetry, imagery, and magic of Christmas have lost their effect on almost everyone. Instead of increasing our dose of reality to the point where it hurts and heals, the traditional poetry, imagery, and magic of Christmas dilutes the message and dims the lights of revelation. Christmas has escaped us. It is infinitely worth stripping Christmas down to its bare essentials and paying close attention to the unbearable reality of the mystery itself. Not the mystery, not the stories, the titles, the poetry, the imagery, but the *mystery itself*, a mystery which is wholly unbearable without the grace of God.

We must relocate Bethlehem to where it belongs: the desert. It can only be reached, as the Magi found, by a long journey across the desert guided by the star of faith. What is it the Magi found at the heart of their long journey? They found Love; they found that love of the quality embodied in Christ is the most real, the most important element in the world. Bethlehem claims that Jesus the Christ is the deepest probe into the meaning of everything. For in him we reach rock bottom, and there is no other. What we see on the surface is history. But in Jesus we see what lies at the center. In Jesus, the reality of the entire universe breaks through.

Chapter Five

The Fullness of Life

No person or tradition has ever come up with a better way of dying, of defeating the ego, than the practice of poverty, chastity, and obedience, which are not principals of opposition to evil but expressions of a higher choice. The dynamic interplay of these virtues may be better understood if we translate these almost hackneyed words into their simplest and deepest meaning. Poverty means *no fuss*. Chastity means *no lust*. And Obedience means *no rust*.

The *poor* person takes God so seriously they take everything else lightheartedly. Drawn and captivated by Christ into the depths of reality, they cannot possible trifle. They lose themselves in the mystery of God.

They become champions of the rights of God and forget all about their own problems. They take good care of God's world and hold nothing cheap. It is their detachment from things that enables them to be great lovers of God and his whole creation.

The chaste man or woman is at least as sexual and ardent as anyone. They don't grab or yearn to possess. They let the people they love go free and become more and more liberated themselves. They have learned to see and pass on. They are one-joy people, wanting everything all at once—i.e. God, in the eternal now, and nothing apart from or less than that. They can only rest in God. But God, especially, is too good to be used. What does one do with God? One celebrates. A sexual symbolic celebration won't do. There is the Eucharist. And the prayer of ecstasy. The monk's (everyone's) whole life is adoration.

The one who is obedient does not subserviently do someone else's will. They are so acutely alive to all possible disclosures of the divine will that no rust could ever accumulate in their perceptive powers. *Obedire* means "to listen." The obedient one is a good listener. From all eternity, says John of the Cross, God speaks one word, and the word reaches its fullness in Christ. The obedient one listens to the word with all of their might, all the time. They absorb, assimilate, and digest it, becoming the word themselves. They listen so intently that they are, like Christ, "obedient unto death, even death on a cross" (Philippians 2:8).

The opposite of listening is *not* listening, or *deafness*. The Latin word is *absurdus*. If we are not obedient, we are absurd. The existentialists err when they cavalierly consider the world absurd; they are absurd themselves because they have not learned to listen with their whole being to the Word. A listening, as T. S. Eliot says, so deep that they become the music while the music lasts.

Donald Amireault, a Nova Scotia priest, once told me, "We all have two ears and one mouth because we're meant to listen twice as hard." This is what Saint Benedict meant when he said we must listen "with the ears of the heart." When we hear the word in our hearts, it "sends us." That's the meaning of the word "apostle."

God does not speak in a vacuum or pull vocations out of hats. We need an abbot or a guru. Obedience means loving listening to another—to all the others—for the sake of the Wholly Other. Virtuous obedience is diametrically opposed to the regimentation of military obedience. It is an artful discipline.

The word discipline derives from the same root as the word disciple, the student who lovingly listens to his teacher. The word pupil is similar. It denotes the black circle in the eye, or a little child in school. Why is the same word used for both? Because the pupil looks into the eyes of the teacher and beholds the reflection of himself. The pupil is the intent looker, seeker, and listener, who absorbs the spirit of the teacher and does what the teacher wants even before the teacher opens his mouth. *Pupila* means little doll. What you see in the eyes of the teacher is a little doll that must become a mature, full-fledged, free person. That requires a great deal of trust. Saint Benedict said that obedience must be *sine murmuratione*. There is no good translation for *murmuratione*, but it means basically, we must obey without grumbling. In other words, there's a close connection between stillness, silence, and obedience. They must always go together.

Through poverty, chastity, and obedience, the mystic dies daily. Death strips man of all external possessions; the mystic anticipates this stripping by being content with the bare necessities of life (poverty). Death deprives man of his biological vitality; the celibate mystic freely fasts and deprives himself of sexual intercourse (chastity). Death means the end of man's pretend independence; the mystic sheds such a pretense by depending on the Church, or more specifically, on a spiritual director (obedience).

By choosing death now, freely and deliberately, letting it come when it may, the mystic draws from that confrontation radical consequences for life really lived, creatively, exuberantly, divinely.

Chapter Six

An Introduction to Prayer

We have spoken of the sheer mercy and joy that God makes available to us. One way to capture this precious abundance is through prayer. We know that, but what we're not so keen about knowing is how and when to pray, how to be sure we have made the capture, recognized it for what it is, and found the way to turn on the spigot for God's response. We know too that there may be times when the answer is delivered under the wings of birds that take the scenic route to get here, or it comes in bits and pieces that we have to put together to make divine sense of them. It's special delivery but not the kind we and the Postal Service are more or less accustomed to.

There are lots of excellent books on prayer written by eminent authors. And don't forget the Gospels. We need to be mindful of the way we spend our day, and note the following: We do not pray in order to have a good day. We have a good day in order to pray. And the numinous is the end, not the means. Though we have many routes to the prayer loft available to us, we need only one word to describe the essence of prayer. Prayer is adoration. We adore Thee. We adore Thee in rapt attention. We adore Thee with all our heart, all our mind, all our sensibility. Adoration is indeed the essence of prayer, and it takes us back to what we said about holiness. Holiness comes from deep relatedness. We said that we can discern what happens when "we are deeply related to one another and to the One who sustains us by His love." The prerequisite to adoration is deep meditation. Yes, be ready for deepness to enjoy these encounters. But the good news is we can attain holy relatedness without making a solitary prostration before a tabernacle real or imagined. And, once attained, that buoyant condition is portable.

The importance of prayer manifests itself in all our activities and in whatever conversations and discussions we undertake, providing we are mindful of our relatedness. The Evangelist Mark relates how Jesus mills with the people he encounters on the road, giving solace to the grieving, advice to the confused, renewal to the injured or diseased, and then goes off to a hidden spot to address his Father. We recognize that latter move as prayer time. Indeed it was, but so were those other meetings and greetings that preceded it. We relate, we attend and listen, we reflect, and finally comes the adoration, the essence of prayer.

Puer Christus[45]

On the feast of Saint Augustine, "prince of Mystics," I was released from the hospital after an episode of congestive heart failure. I went for a walk on Carlsbad Beach, gratefully aware of the beauty, power, and permanence of the ocean. I was still absorbed introspectively, ruminating on my own human diminishment and on the intensified struggle of my own brave little band of Carmelite contemplatives.

Rising out of the water is primordial. History, science, religion, combat, literature, the arts, and, of course, evolution and sheer human and animal enjoyment depend on this aquatic experience. It has a lot to do with our sexuality—our own vast sea and its tidal waves of energy. It is all so wondrous. It is massive and magical, the largest source of our dread and delight. The surface of the earth is mostly water, and it dominates us. The mystery of the sea, whether in Galilee or Hawaii, threatens us and fascinates us. We can

---

[45] McNamara, William. 2006. Chapter 4, "The Human Adventure" IN: *Wild and Robust*. Cambridge, Massachusetts: Cowley Publications. 293 pp.

never master this terrible force but must cope with it creatively, cooperatively, and awesomely. Our own erotic sea is the same—all this beauty and power require from us a degree of individual ingenuity that will enable us to be so personally and uniquely sexual that the oceanic megalosaurus will not incapacitate us.

Aphrodite, the goddess of sexual love, has limitations. All she can do is make introductions, establish connection. Then we must traverse our way through the delirious and dolorous phases of human intimacy and, ultimately, of divine union. This is called sexual intelligence.

It has taken me nearly a full page to say that. But on the beach one day in Carlsbad, California, I realized it in only a moment, in a religious experience. Externally, hardly anything happened—a boy, exuding health and happiness, radiating youthful ardor and hope, rising out of the sea with his surfboard, yelled across the beach to me with a vibrant, cheerful "hi" and passed on into whatever, leaving his mark on me for all eternity. My whole being resonated with the heartbeat of all reality, namely *Puer Christus*, Boy Christ.

Surfing has always been my favorite analogy of the ascetical-mystical life, of the balance of human existence. Surfing is a series of disciplined acts, or asceticism, followed by ecstasy or mysticism. Here you have a perfect combination of two basic human impulses: dread and delight. Note the discipline as the surfer gets up early in the morning, polishes his board, and carries it expectantly toward the sea. There he faces an empty beach and aqueous immensity and confronts the cold, raging waves. Arduously he paddles out into the deeps. Capping this whole assiduous glissando, he waits with the patience of a cat, looking, sniffing, and scanning the horizon, not lackadaisically for any old wave, but contemplatively for the perfect one.

Waiting is his secret and his genius, and the results are lusciously rewarding. Eventually the surfer spots the longed-for wave, rumbling toward him with exquisite power and majesty. He moves deftly and adroitly into position and takes the wave at its rampant momentum, then relaxes, resonates and rides, rides, and rides—sheer ecstasy, the delicious fruit of contemplative, discipline mindfulness, God suffusing and animating this pinnacle of action.

Mystical life is a carefully crafted balance between two polarities: 1) don't just stand there, do something, and 2) don't just do something, stand there. One without the other is inhuman. Unless God alone knocks us off balance, it is our indispensable obligation to develop a deliberate harmonious self, interrelating reverently with others, God, and the universe. Our own

growth will be authentic only if we learn to unite asceticism and mysticism, discipline and delight, suffering and celebration. Only this smooth and undulating
rhythm of life engenders human wholeness, holiness,
and uproarious happiness.

Chapter Seven

Meditation II: Meeting the Samaritan Woman

Who was this man who strode like a giant across the land who we call "holy"? Up and down mountains he went, hunkering down in desert places for simple nourishment—natural and supernatural—for conversation with his small band of followers, telling stories, jokes, parables, and making plans on how to live fully and love deeply in a society half dead from the stifling burdens of legalism and moralism. These sessions with his chosen friends always crackled with humor, crucial insights, and refreshing laughter. No one ever spoke like this man. And no one could penetrate your hidden self with such piercing eyes as this monumental master of primordial words and the terrible truth.

Who was this man who went in and out of tides, in and out of crowds, in and out of trouble, of danger, of traps set by men of fear, power, and prestige? With what seemed like a perfect combination of ferocity and jocosity, he dismissed his enemies while he fascinated and charmed everyone else. With a cavalier sangfroid he broke worn-out laws and worn-down hearts. Silliness and stuckness seemed to repel him so he strove quietly and lovingly to make all things new. If massive means did not achieve desirable goals, why clutter your life with them? Fanatics multiply means to an end peremptorily, without ever reaching said end. The Scribes and Pharisees multiplied trivial laws and mindless ritual with no right or religious experience, with no resonance of deity and therefore nothing to express.

Extremes of piety on the one hand, whatever is showy and phony on the other; all that is bland and boring. Because every creature in its awesome particularity enchanted him, he was exquisitely sensitive to earthly conditions and human situations. Though there was something wild and raw about him—scary at times—he was sensitive about his own cosmic, theandric personality, about his call, his destiny and his Father's will. Psychologists today would call him narcissistic. How absurd! When he was exposed to excruciating pain and shame what he suffered from most of all was not the wounds from whips and nails, but from the betrayal of his friends. Because he was a colossal lover they were stunned, and in shocking, shameful cowardice whispered to one another, "Maybe he is sick." In the face of his heroic deeds they felt keenly their own solipsistic sassiness and could do nothing but slink away.

His donkey did not abandon him. He kicked away the tombstone, entered the death chamber, licked and warmed the body of his loving master who rose up and rode the donkey out of the deadly darkness into the light of day and into the incandescent presence of Mary Magdalene, one of the women he loved. The newness he longed for, the fire he was determined to ignite would begin here, as the Kingdom, the resurrected order of being, erupted between them. Were there even greater lovers than this? This was the inception of the I-Thou philosophy. I-It would no longer be tolerable. Individuals can still survive on an I-It relationship but not persons—not authentic human beings. From now on dialogue will prevail. We will be erotic or robots, saints or sanctimonious studs.

I say it began here. Yes, with a heightened tide of passion to be sustained forever by the inflowing power of the Holy Spirit. Jesus, this most manly man, was moved by the Spirit to become the most erotic man in the history of the world. After all, his father, whose will he came to do, was Eros. He embodied and transmitted that infinite, boundless love. Every "other" was a "Thou" to him. Jesus himself was, as St. Francis de Sales said, "God in his most attractive form."

A spectacular instance of all this is found in the Gospel of John. As Martin Buber insists, "all real living is meeting"—meeting in depth. A profound act of mindful communion. One time Jesus had to leave Judea and go to Galilee. This meant that he had to go through Samaria. So he took a deep breath and, all alone, departed for Samaria. Jacob's well was there so he headed for that. Tired when he arrived, he sat on the well and rested. This happened at six o'clock. Whenever John wants to emphasize the importance of an event, he mentions the specific time.

And though he was thirsty after his journeying, Jesus did not draw any water. This is interesting. Obviously, he anticipated an encounter and so did not want to spoil it by a premature and impetuous act. Meeting is far more urgent than drinking. And, sure enough, in a few minutes the Samaritan woman arrived eager to draw water. Jesus addressed her simply and straightforwardly, "Will you give me a drink?" It's almost a typical pub scene in Sligo, Boston, Los Angeles, or Milwaukee. An Erosphere suffuses the whole contextual situation. The moral splendor and spiritual audacity that Jesus brings to the meeting is incomparable. Otherwise the scene in Sligo is very similar to the one in Samaria. Boundaries are broken, interior depths are revealed. Desires are heightened.

The woman raises the question about the traditional hostility between Jews and Samaritans. Jesus simply ignored the problem as if it were too petty to be recognized. He is concerned about one thing only, and that is that she recognizes living water when she sees it and longs for nothing more than it and the fullness of life it represents.

The Samaritan woman is on the verge of belief now but still wonders. To paraphrase: you seem like a prophet but certainly not greater than our father, Jacob, who gave us this well and drank from it himself. Jesus's answer is shockingly wonderful. Usually reticent about his divine nature he becomes, in loving dialogue with this strange but alluring woman, generously revealing. Jacob's water is fine, he said, but it won't slake your thirst forever. Mine will. I have come to give you everlasting life. He wasn't saying, as he often did, take it or leave it. He felt erotically compelled to enrich and enliven this attractive woman's life. How relieved he was when she gushed, "Give me this water." He cut to the chase by revealing to her, her own life. She was embarrassed but extremely impressed. So relaxed did she become in his centering presence she decided to ask him another burning question. Where does true worship take place—in Jerusalem or Samaria? Neither place is an authentic criterion. Jesus pointed out that as humanity evolves all worship is truth insofar as it is worshipped in spirit and truth. Is it a cry of a heart, a penetrating insight that sees things as they really are? Is it a direct and immediate experience of Christ himself and not just notions about him? Is it the presence of God felt?

Jesus answered all of the questions for the Samaritan woman. She felt his love and knew he cared. What a sexy man, she thought, who is obviously a prophet, in fact, the Messiah! She ran back home and told everyone that she met a pure, erotic lover. She knew he was the Son of God.

John shows in his first epistle how the whole Christian apostolate began with a mystical experience. He sees the passion and the resurrection as the inevitable outcome of a mystical life. Since John, Christianity has become hideously subverted.

Who will restore radical Christianity by a worldwide renewal of the church's mystical life? Karl Rahner said if it does not happen the Church is worth nothing at all. This conviction is, in fact, shared by an informed majority.

Chapter Eight

A Cry of the Heart[46]

C hristian Humanism is a worldwide perspective that is neither liberal nor conservative, neither relative nor absolute, neither fixed securely in lapidary dogmas nor floating lackadaisically in far fantasies. Though steeped in science and sustained by the arts, Christian Humanism is larger than both; though inspired by the Christian experience and enlightened by other reliable religious traditions, it exceeds them while integrating them seriously and creatively, acknowledging their value with pungency and enthusiasm. A humanism that is merely secular is hardly a genuine humanism.

---

[46] From *The Human Experience: A Divine Madness.* 2010. McNamara

Any ideology that divides the human race into <u>us</u> and <u>them</u> is not an authentic humanism. A belief system that regards a select segment of humanity as either chosen or superhuman is not humanistic—neither is ethnocentrism, chauvinism, anti-Semitism, radical feminism, or homophobia. If we are actively convinced of our interfused relationships to all creatures on earth, and nothing is foreign to or independent of our love and care, then our spirituality may be called cosmic or planetary, and our lifestyle a fulgent instance of Christian Humanism.

"Christian" does not introduce an exclusive note, but rather a universal principle, a unifying presence. The world belongs to God, not us. We are responsible stewards, or, if you will, high priests of creation. If we love God, we love his world. Christ is the embodiment of this love—of the Infinite, the Ineffable. "He who sees me," Jesus said, "sees the Father," the Origin, the Source, the Erotic Energy, the Unifying One who is always there. And the ravishing marvel is that the Holy Other is there, here, everywhere—infinitely distinct, super-personal, but utterly, unspeakably human.

In the rhythm of life and its evolution, at the center of the cosmos in the world, there is a divine center, a living heart, beating with the fierce and fiery energy of Eros and pathos—prodigious care (Eros) and painful involvement (pathos). It is basic and therefore simple: all in Christ and Christ in all. If I lost my faith in the invisible, the intangible, I would cling tenaciously to the word and to the flesh, knowing that matter matters and where there is flesh, there is spirit. The concentration of living, breathing matter, in the heart of the flesh, symbolizes the very core of spirit.

There is nothing like the Incarnation of God to shake us out of our humdrum everydayness. Our contemporary problem is banality, a bland, boring disorder that can be vanquished by only one thing: carnality infused with spirit. De Chardin, a religious scientist mystic and audacious human lover, protects devotion to the Sacred Heart from pietistic claptrap and sentimental schlock. The incarnate spirituality of divinized matter and flesh, of hallowing heaven and earth, of crucified love, of sheer loyalty—this is real Christianity, and it keeps the world from falling apart.

The most popular of Catholic devotions calls the dynamic central force, this diffusive energy, the Sacred Heart. Unfortunately, like so many popular devotions, it tends to be sentimental, often spurious, even Pecksniffian. But De Chardin, a Jesuit Priest, mystic, and scientist, captures in his *Phenomenon of Man* the fascinating, thrilling, shocking reality of the Sacred Heart. Christ's heart became for him the powerful image of God's outpouring love and life pulsating through the whole of creation. That small, fleshy human heart embodied a fire animating the whole world.

Jesus was passionately pure and purely passionate. He was led by the spirit directly to the end, to the Other; following him means risking our lives for the other. Genuine otherness evokes from the *yearning* lover three riveting, reverent acts of contemplation: aspiration, appreciation, and adoration. *Aspiration* drives us beyond satisfaction to something that endures faithfully and permeates deeply. *Appreciation* is so delightful; it pleases and gratifies us forever. *Adoration* catapults us out of our separate existence into union with the other.

This is what Jesus taught his friends when, out of a felt need, they asked him how to pray. Prayer is a cry of the heart, ultimately the cry of the sacred heart of Christ. Think of the whole world crying out of an immense sea of sorrow or out of Olympian joy, the universal cry of the deer, the wolf, the coyote, the lion, the dog and cat, the donkey, the horse, the seal, and the loon; think of old men and young girls, of lonely individuals and mindless crowds. Of refugees and prisoners, of triumphant athletes and multitudes of the sick and the insane. Then think of the Representative Man, the High Priest of creation, who hangs on the cross, gathers up all these tiny fragments of prayer, the cries of the heart, and unites them with his own infinite and ultimate cry: "My God, My God, why have you forsaken me?" (Mt 27:46)

This terrible, tormented scream from the cross, was followed by the most triumphant human howl in the history of the world: "It is done!" What exactly was accomplished? His glorious passion; his passionate life, lustrous and radiant, culminating in his torture by way of the cross on Calvary, fulfilled in his stunning victory over death. After his donkey kicked away the stone from his tomb, the Representative Man, the God Man rose and rode, gleaming with divine dignity, smiting his beloved, Magdalena, with unbearable, untouchable love, and gathering his feckless, fearful disciples into an unflinching commitment and unfailing solidarity. His cry became their cry, and the panting, sweating, soaring Church came into existence and to this day, though beaten and ashamed, remains indomitable. How come? Because the spirit, Eros, enlivens and dynamizes the worldly saint and the touched sinners. And the one salvific cry of the Sacred Heart sanctifies us all despite how oppressed we are by absurdity, banality, and ignorance. Sanctify us? Well yes, if we resemble him in our own unique way as faithful lovers. Jesus did not want fans. He wanted robust followers.

Christ's cry of the heart is called the "Our Father," and that's what he taught the disciples. The concept of God as "Our Father" was already prevalent in Jewish piety centuries before Christ. Jesus simply intensified this central concept. In the Jewish tradition, God is the father of a family, a people in covenant with him, a covenant of obedience to his will. In the Gospels, the disciples of Jesus are the family, the people with whom God makes a new covenant. The word "father" is full of love and affection. But the New Testament is unique and revolutionary when it uses "Our Father" as a personal address to God. Never before was the Holy One called *Abba*. Modern exegetes have made the most of this newfound "daddy" tenderness in the Deity. A plethora of the populace have turned the Ineffable into a soft and indulgent God who is infinite sweetness to them, offering comfort and solace in all circumstances. So the Christian challenge is gone and with it, the loss of awe, wonder, holy fear, and radical astonishment.

Jesus's own understanding of *Abba*, Father, was quite different: absolute love, truly intimate and involved, but transcendent and unbearable except for grace. When we pray we enter into the cave of a lion all right, and we do not know if we will come out alive. We must go in, otherwise there is no intimacy, ecstasy, or fecundity; but we go in appropriately only if we are ontologically fearful; that is, reverent, humble, repentant, and ready for total ego annihilation.

The Gospel concept of the father-son relationship was influenced by Jewish culture. The son had no life or even existence of his own. All was the father's. The son owed him complete, unconditional obedience. Jesus was the perfect example of this. He claimed nothing for himself. He came from the Father and was returning to the Father.

In the meantime, Jesus has only one criterion for everything: his Father's will. Our following Christ means identifying with his living for the Father. It means being nourished for that carefree, God-centered life by the same wellsprings that fed Jesus. When we are nourished on this food, we rarely need psychotherapy. Jesus does not come to coo but to share with us his vision, his passionate dedication to the Father's will. He inspires, instills his pluck, ignites fervor, and braces us for the crucial situations and life's momentous task.

Our Father

All this is contained in the Our Father prayer. If we really pray it mindfully, absorbingly, then we think like God by putting on the mind of Christ. But this seldom happens. We hardly know what we are saying and what we mean when we recite the prayer mindlessly. No matter how gravid with spirit a prayer is, when we repeat the Our Father as often as we have, it is liable to become rote, recited with no deep conviction, no inspiration, no uplifting worship and no religious experience.

Therefore, a suggestion: pray the Our Father backwards—not word by word, but petition after petition from the end to the beginning. It seems to make more sense that way, at least existentially. When I do it, the experience unfolds differently each time but essentially in the following manner.

The first petition from the back end is *Deliver us from evil.* We desperately need to be liberated, to be rescued, to be transformed. We need a redeemer. We are stuck in evil, so subtly submerged in it that we hardly recognize it. We let too many things happen. We get used to living insouciantly in a calamitous and decadent situation. I am not referring to outrageous, appalling deeds of a criminal nature. I mean *pretty poisons*, the respectable kind of evil that killed Christ. Big bad men didn't do it. Pretty poison did. Pretty poison is the kind of infection that seeps unnoticeably into our nicest people and our best institutions. It permeates our culture. The poison is potent precisely because it is so pretty.

The Aramaic scriptures were translated into Greek. Three different words were used to indicate three particular kinds of evil. The one used in the Our Father was *poneros*, conveying a very specific evil. It means "hard labor" with no significance—the kind criminals are condemned to. Little rocks are made out of big rocks simply to pass the time, without purpose or meaning. We don't need to go to prison to experience this. Most lives, and the jobs that fill them, are equally meaningless. It is from this we beg to be delivered.

Lead us not into temptation, the next petition, is not a request to be spared all temptation. That would make our lives dull and bland. We need to be tempted, challenged and provoked. So we pray to be delivered from those temptations we don't need in order to confront with focused energy the very temptations we cannot live without.

Forgive us our trespasses as we forgive those who trespass against us. This is a crucial petition. It's like crossing the Red Sea. What a responsible prayer! We are not simply seeking forgiveness; we want pardon only to the extent that we forgive others. Forgiveness is freedom. We get rid of all the baggage that clutters the interior and makes us sluggish and lethargic. The trick is to take God so seriously that we take ourselves and our little world lightheartedly. There is no hardness of heart in a God-centered, lighthearted person.

The Bread Of Tomorrow

Give us today the bread of tomorrow. This petition was not understood until a century ago. No one (not even Origen and Saint Jerome who were pioneer scripture scholars) knew what the Greek word *epiousios* meant. This word appears nowhere else in literature. Only recently did new archeological digs, new discoveries, and hard exegetical work shed light on the word and, therefore, on the meaning of the petition. We are praying for *epiousios* bread, symbolic bread, the bread of tomorrow. We are praying for the *eschaton*, that personal, direct encounter with Christ, knowing once that happens, we will never be the same again. We were created and are graced for that momentous experience.

There is a tendency in us to deal with God indirectly; to pose, to fabricate, to postpone and hide like Adam and Eve. We want to be warmed by the fire who is Christ but never consumed. Yet we are aware of our restless hearts, our loneliness, our dissatisfaction, the absence of ultimate, intimate Presence, of spousal union. God invites us again and again into this final communion. The no's we come up with are uncanny: polite, respectable, polished, and imaginative. But they are a sham and worse than a sham: our pretty poisonous way of saying "Crucify him, crucify him!" The invitation persists, and so does the fierce ontological ache of our shriveled existence.

To experience the eschaton is to look into the eyes and heart of the Divine Lover, Infinite Eros, and as in a mirror, to behold ourselves, as we are now and as we were meant to be. This encounter is not way off, way out there, at the end of our lives. It is here and now, so we pray that it happens today. Only then can we really mean the next prayer.

Thy will be done on earth as it is in heaven. Who can say this prayer and mean it? We need lots of *epiousios* bread. We need trust and courage. We need authenticity. But if enough ardent souls really prayed this petition, we could change the world.

Thy Kingdom come. The Our Father is a genuine cry of the heart, utterly existential, and therefore magnificent and magnanimous. And it cannot be thus without being significantly political-mystical. "Thy Kingdom come." That's all that matters. Oh Thou! Forget the I, the me, the my and the mine. All I want is you; not a version of you, a theology, a prayer, a spiritual path or a worldview. I want you, and therefore, your Kingdom. Establish your reign in the world. Let there be justice and peace and above all, love. Whatever of me or mine impedes your reign, take from me. If I myself am obtrusive or preoccupied with something other than your Kingdom, your perfect love, then slay me.

Hallowed be thy name. There is hardly anything sacred in this secular world. Times and places have been flattened and made to serve our utilitarian purposes. But the Name of God is so intrinsically holy, so immutably good, that nothing can extinguish it. Be hallowed. Be holy. Be God in our Godless society. Be a luminous, refulgent presence in our dark, dull midst. Be pure passion and pathos in our apathetic, frantic business. Be a harbor of stillness in the midst of our media madness. Save the disgraceful shambles of our language—profaned, humiliated, and vulgarized—by the rumbling thunder of your Word.

Thou who art in heaven. We are almost ready to pronounce the words which alone constitute the essence of prayer. But we must not botch it, so we set the stage and refine our disposition, branding our worship with awe, alterity, and adoration.

Our God is not a nice or comfy thing to be possessed, amused, palliated, or manipulated. He is not a mascot, an uncle, or a teddy bear. He is an earthquake. He does not fit into our pocket, our mind, or our earth. He is in heaven. He is transcendent. He is Wholy Other. He designs our destiny and enables us to achieve it. WE become miserable—and the infection spreads— when we try to control our own lives and be our own captains. How silly to expect God to be the kind of God we want. We cannot pave a way for ourselves; the Spirit must lead us. Choosing our own path conveniently is always egregious folly.

"In heaven" means that God transcends our natural boundaries. It is up to God to reveal himself. Jesus proves the trustworthiness of God. He lives out of one basic conviction: God is love. This love is a force, a fire, a father, a mother, a spouse. God makes high proposals of love and devastating demands.

We need to be irrevocably committed to Jesus. We need to remain faithful. If we break the bond, we break his heart and his body on earth. We need to base our lives on his dark knowledge of the Father. There is no other way. Some try to drag Jesus onto a path made garish by natural human lights. We absurdly try to dictate to God his providence. We are actually with God in heaven. We see the tip of the iceberg on earth. There, too, we see the tip of human consciousness. The deeper and more real self is hidden "in heaven" with Christ, where everything is related directly and immediately to the Father. Apart from his exquisitely tender, fierce love, nothing makes sense.

Now the mental stage is set. Having prayed the other prayers from bottom to top, we are now carefully disposed and ready to say the perfect prayer with an informed and enchanted sense of the Holy: *Our Father*.

Chapter Nine

Confession and the Vital Experience of Mercy

He offered me a gourmet dinner
which I accepted with magnificent
glee and joyful gratitude. While he
himself served me, despite a happy
noisy crowd, I said to this efferves-
cent adopted son of Josephine
Baker, "She was a saint." He re-
sponded with alarming excitement,
"Oh, no! She was a sinner!"
I know what he meant --

One of my favorite contemporary philosophers is Jacob Needleman, who teaches at the San Francisco State University. He wrote a book called *The Heart of Philosophy* (1982). He said that he teaches philosophy daily to his students but that philosophy never does any good. It's useless until, on rare occasions, a philosophical idea sinks down into the heart and...*catches fire.* Then he realizes that all his work and all his teaching are worthwhile. The whole thing has become existential.

Let me share with you some of my own reflections on sin and reconciliation, the sacrament of penance, and suggest a rather specific way of doing it, of confecting[47] the sacrament as priest and penitent. Albert Camus, the illustrious French philosopher, said that the basic philosophical question was suicide. I think that's close.

The worst sins are sins of the spirit. And of the spirit, the worst sins are sins against love, sins against charity—always a betrayal of love. When you hear confessions, most of the sins you hear are rather bodily sins, fleshy sins, and sins that are committed by mistake, by human weakness—momentary sins. No one, almost no one is ever in confession to address the disorientation of a whole human life, nor the subtleties and banalities and puerilities that characterize that wayward existence, that absurdity, that foolishness.

We don't have to have poignantly tangible feelings, in the plural. We may not even cry. That's not necessary. In fact, sorrow is sometimes so deep that

---

[47] "To put together by combining materials" (www.the-freedictionary.com/confecting)

one doesn't detect it in the shallow aspects of the human personality, in the emotions. So there are no *feelings* of sorrow. But there is a deep down conviction that one has disturbed the universe, that one has hurt another human being. Which is a terrible thing. Remember what the fathers of the church used to say: be kind, be kind, be kind and you will be a saint.

We are in bad shape. But we are also imbued with power from on high. We are endowed with Christ's life in Christ love. We are drenched in his mercy. So we do not cope with sin by suicide or escape, but by thrusting ourselves completely and totally on God's mercy: in, through, and with Christ. Not on our own accomplishments or achievements, and not on our job or the efficacy of our job. But alone on God's mercy.

Not long ago a big corporation in New York gathered together its leaders and sent them to a conference. And the leader of the conference asked them to dissociate themselves from their job. He said, "Prescind[48] entirely from your job, and then evaluate yourself as a human being from one to ten. How human are you? How real are you? How satisfied are you with life? How much do you enjoy it? That sort of thing." On a scale of one to ten, no one rated himself more than one. Most zero. Apart from their jobs, they were nothing. So that's what we have got to watch out for.

---

[48] "Separate yourself" (www.thefreedictionary.com/prescind)

And that's the kind of sinfulness that we slip into through pretty poison. We forget God. We are not God-conscious. We are not Christ-conscious. <u>What think ye of Christ?</u> That's the greatest Christian question, the essential Christian question. And once you know him, you fall in love with him. And once you love him, you practice all the virtues. So maybe one of our greatest sins is not knowing Christ and not reading, rereading the life of Christ over and over again, penetrating with perceptive appreciation who God is, enfleshed, embodied in the Christ. And not only the historical, but the mystical and the cosmic Christ, the whole Christ, discovering and rediscovering him, and so moving into deeper and deeper realms of love, willing to be spent.

What you see on the crucifixes is one who is spent—totally, unselfconsciously, without bargaining or reservation, spent for you, and for me. Loving self-sacrifice, that's life, that's living. So the big sin may be the opposite of self-sacrifice: being safe, being comfortable, being secure, being in many manifold ways selfish. So those are the kinds of sins we have to come to terms with. But we should never, never be glum, or we should never give up, because of Christ.

The greatest lesson is Peter. The wonderful thing is that of all the apostles, Peter is the one who actually sinned the most as far as we can tell from the Gospel story. Peter seemed to be the weakest, the most impulsive. And yet he is the one whom Jesus chose to be his pope, his vicar on earth, his rock. Why? Well, obviously Jesus really loved him and loved him for particular reasons. Two things occur to me. One, he was always willing to go out on a limb for Christ. And that's what our Lord needed. He didn't need any kind of grumpy rectitude. He didn't need an upright middle-class man. He needed a follower who loved him and took chances and took risks to follow him. And Peter did that. So Jesus loved him.

The other thing that I find remarkable about Peter is his bounce. It's the bounce that counts. And so Peter was able to fall off that branch and fall again and again. But he had this bounce. He had humility. Someone asked one of the saints what the basic virtue was, and the saint said there are three: humility, humility, and humility. And that is true. Charity is the greatest of all the virtues. And faith is the key. But the basis, the foundation is humility: the real consciousness of ourselves as creatures, as sinners, and as people who are loved and saved and redeemed and turned into Christ by God's Holy Spirit. If we let him. If we are docile. If we are repentant every day of our lives. If we get out of the way. There will be nothing left to impede the divine rapture.

Remember how Christ warned Peter that he would commit the most terrible sin? He would deny, in a crunch, that he even knew him. We very often do that unwittingly, silently, culturally in our lives, without saying anything. Jesus said, "you will deny me when the cock crows" and Peter did. It was the terrible, ultimate moment in the life of Peter. And he could have done what Judas did. But instead he relied on Jesus's mercy. He knew that Jesus was sheer mercy, sheer love.

I often think of the two Irish women, Mary and Sheila. Mary was trying to talk her out of the drink and asked, "What will you say to Peter when you reach the Gate of Heaven?" And Sheila said, "I'll look him straight in the eye and I'll say cock-a-doodle-do!" We may need to do that, too. And it's a wonderful thing to do because we're simply reminding God of his favorite daily miracle, his mercy. There is nothing he would rather be than merciful, and it's only to sinners he can show mercy.

The bad thing is not that we are sinners; the bad thing is not allowing God to redeem us, and to touch and caress and heal us in our sinfulness. So what we've got to be is just *touched sinners*, and that's all we can be. That's what Saints are, touched sinners. They allow God to touch them. Sometimes we get so rigid and frigid and self-conscious we lose confidence, lose respect for ourselves because there's so much sin; then we don't allow God to forgive us.

This appeal for God-consciousness comes to you from a priest, yes, but a priest who is also a penitent.

And this sacrament like all the others depends on a human principle. Recall that Saint Thomas said grace perfects nature. The efficacy of the sacraments depends upon that principle. Grace perfects nature. So the sacrament will be as good as it is *natural*. And one of the reasons that sacraments don't work too well, *ex opera operantis*[49], is that they are not confected very well, very naturally, humanly, thoughtfully, lovingly.

Priests, after doing the sacraments for years and years, might tend to become automatic, routine and mindless. And that robs the sacrament of a great deal of vitality, a lot of healing, saving power. Something happens. I would dare say, for instance, in this sacrament of penance that almost all the time, no matter how badly confected by both priest and penitent, there is grace there. The confessional is not a sin bin, it is the grace place. And so there is grace, and it is fructified to some extent. But it depends upon how fertile the sacrament is. Most of the time it works. People get

---

[49] Due to the priest or recipient…"A technical term literally meaning 'from the work of the doer,' to be distinguished from *ex opere operato*, which refers to the grace-conferring power inherent in the sacramental rite itself, as an action of Christ. *Ex opere operantis* refers to the role and value of the recipient's or minister's moral condition in causing or receiving sacramental grace." (www.encyclopedia.com/religion/encyclopedias-almanacs-transcripts-and-maps/ex-opere-operantis)

rid of the sin. But that's just the negative effect of the sacrament.

The positive effect of this sacrament is transformation into Christ. Now, that almost never happens. So although we're good enough, just barely good enough as priests, as confessors, to help get rid of people's sins, we are not good enough at all. We don't confect the sacrament humanly enough, mindfully enough, really respecting the penitent, being deeply moved so that the person goes out of the reconciliation room, out of the sacrament transformed—thinking, loving, acting more like Christ. That seldom happens.

Now it's very interesting that since Vatican II lots of change in the church has occurred. But these changes most often occurred after a lot of study of the document of Vatican II, and a lot of discussion, discourse, dialogue among the theologians. In regard to the Sacrament of Penance, on the other hand, there was none. People just stopped going to confession, including perhaps most all priests and religious sisters, even though lawfully required to go every two weeks. And people in general hardly go. Why? Because it was obvious to them that confession was not being done very humanly. There was no good, natural foundation. There was a kind of cheating going on. They would hop in and pop out and make a little recitation of things. And gradually as they became more educated and more sophisticated, I think they came to realize that this couldn't possibly be the way God mercifully redeems and transforms a sinner.

Now, sacramental fecundity depends on the priest. The priest has got to be very intelligent, for one thing. Saint Teresa of Avila shopped around quite a bit for a good confessor. But she said she would prefer an intelligent priest to a pious priest. Some pious priests misled her. And so she got really disturbed with them. There was a period of her life, for instance, when she thought she could, if she advanced high enough, go beyond Jesus, the Christ, and just deal with God as he is in himself. She began to think that and did so for quite a while. Then she found an intelligent confessor who helped her regain her senses and realized that Christ was the Way, the Truth, and the Life, and there's no bypassing him; there's never a goal beyond him. You may not know his name but you intuit an infinite attraction deep inside of you for something more—a compelling invitation into the depths of mystery, into the selfless gift of pure act, into the throbbing heart of sacred otherness.

You go beyond your present images of Christ, and your images become refined, and more refined. So ultimately there seems there is no image. I think there still is, but it's so refined that it seems as if there's no image at all. If we take the best philosophers seriously, people like E. I. Watkin and Heidegger, then we know that we know and love without some kind of exercise of the imagination. So I think that what Saint John of the Cross and Saint Teresa were saying is that the whole process of imaging becomes so refined that the image is no longer an idol, no longer takes the place of the unknowable, ineffable God; we are able to move through that thin vapor, as it were, and see God, as scripture says: through a glass darkly.

As we all know, Satan is subtlety personified. That's what Satan is. And the great tradition of the church is not that Satan is an ogre, a beastly sort of character. Remember when our Lord confronted him how subtle he was? There was a beauty. There was a wit there, and a brilliance, enticing Jesus into things that the ordinary man would relish: economic power, political power, and spiritual power. That's how subtle he was. But Jesus rejected those three temptations.

No causal instance but a colossal effort is required to be carefully intuitive by the grace of God. Remember how extremely subtle Satan was tempting Jesus? It is the same in confession or spiritual direction. Saint Theresa was dissatisfied until she found an intelligent confessor—rare birds according to her. A confessor who could identify the subtleties of Satan.

The priest has got to be contemplative; a good listener, listening with his heart, so that he hears beneath the words of the penitent the ache in the heart, the terrible remorse of a sinner. There's nothing like it in the world. And sometimes you hear the cry of the deer from the woods, of a wounded animal and you think you're going to die, it's just so horrible. Yet the greatest pain in the world is the ache of a sinful heart. It's almost unbearable and would be except for Christ. I find the old adage insufficient: "There but for the grace of God, go I." A deeper truth may be: "There with the grace of God, go I."

In New York City, there's a marvelous place that provides a fantastic service for penance. There are priests in about six boxes in this big church all day long, hearing confessions. And you can go in any time. Even into the night. It's near the train station. It's near the bus station. It's very convenient—like going to a gas station. Unfortunately, it's too much like going to a gas station.

For priests, the service is particularly remarkable. You don't just go into a box. You go into a room. There's a nice chair there, and a table, Bible, coffee pot and prie-dieu. You just sit or kneel down and prepare yourself. When you're ready, you push a button on the wall and a priest pops up. It's fantastic. But what kind of a priest is another question. I've gone there often but never made a good confession. Not my fault.

I remember preparing for a favorite feast, the Transfiguration of Christ. And I hadn't been able to go to confession for a long time. I had been on the road, and I was really looking forward to this. I think a very important part of the feast is going to confession. That's a good criterion, by the way, of when to confess. Going every big feast is better than saying, "I'll go every two weeks," or "every month," at least you do it liturgically. Pope St. Pious X said that the most important teaching tool we have is the liturgical year. And so to confess that way is very good. So never let a significant feast go by.

Anyway, I was preparing for the Transfiguration. So I spent an hour in this little room. Then I pushed the button. Up popped the priest. And it took me about five minutes to unload. When I with great relief finished, he said, "What did you say?" I said, "Just bless me." And another time I went, and the priest sang all during my confession. Softly, sweetly, he sang. And this sort of thing kept happening.

I said to myself, they mustn't hear me. They mustn't be listening. I had to test this. So I did a rather naughty thing. Which is natural. So I went one day and pushed the button. The priest popped up and I said, "Father, I'm a priest, a religious, a monk, an abbot. And I just committed adultery. Then I killed the woman and threw the body into the Hudson." There was a slight pause and then the priest said, "Ah, now, Father, keep up the good work." It's true. Then I knew. They don't listen. Or else the average priest is a pretty interesting person.

In confession, obviously, the priest has got to be very attentive. I'd say that's the key word: attentive. Very attentive, very responsive to the penitent. He doesn't need to arouse tangible expressible sorrow. He just has to set the stage for it, create the environment for real sorrow. Don't let the penitent act inhumanly. Do what Christ did, set the stage for a human encounter. Divine infusion is bound to follow.

Father Murphy was trying to arouse sorrow in his parish, and he was speaking to all the people, and he said, "You've got to remember that this very day any man, woman, or child in this parish could die and face judgement." There was a little man in the front row who kept giggling. But the priest continued trying to arouse sadness and sorrow and fear. So he repeated it. He says, "Did you not hear what I said? This very day any man, woman, or child in this parish could die and face the Almighty Judge." The little man kept giggling. So Father Murphy said, "Did you not hear what I said?" And the wee man said, "Yes, Father I heard, but I'm not in this parish." So it's useless activity, futile, and one ought not even try to do that sort of thing. As I say, it's a basic conviction that you've broken the law, disturbed the universe, pampered or pilloried yourself.

And you have not hit the target. The definition of sin goes all the way back to Aristotle, who said it's missing the target. An inhuman act is missing the target. And then St. Thomas Aquinas picked that up and said, yes, sin is essentially an intellectual mistake. We are so divinely constituted and orientated toward the good that we cannot sin without creating some kind of hallucination or illusion first. It's got to seem an illusion that this limited creature could satisfy the infinite hunger and thirst of a human being. Only limitless being can do that.

Only limitless being can satisfy and fulfill the yearnings of a human being.

So that's the fact. Only limitless being can satisfy and fulfill the yearnings of a human being. We are so bent and twisted that we get disoriented and misguided, and so we say, well, maybe this person or this food or this experience or this pleasure, maybe this will satisfy me, fulfill me. There is no limited being that can do that. Or, if you gather together twelve million beings, they can't fulfill you. Only limitless being. Only God can. And so, of course, God is offended if we are addicted to these little creatures, to limited being. Or that we express autonomy, act as if we had the right to say what is right, what is wrong, what is good, what is bad, instead of keeping the law until it turns into love. Love is the law. But we've got to feed on the baby food until the law is kept. The purpose of the law is to free us. Once freed—Christened—the law slips away and we are left with enlightened, obedient love. Just how forceful is now indubitably clear. The Gospel and

Saint Paul's letters are on to this basic truth. Subsequently, no one spells it out, distills and elaborates it as deftly as does Saint John of the Cross. So do secular writers such as Dostoevsky, Tolstoy, Kazantzakis, Walker Percy, and Caryll Houselander.

Now a few suggestions about how and how not to confess:

Some of you may want to go to confession. I suggest that first of all you don't resort to euphemisms. Euphemism: a nice word for a terrible deed. Like the woman who confessed she wasn't nice to her husband. She had bumped him off. She didn't want to say that she killed him. She resorted to euphemism. Don't do that. If you kill someone, say so, confess it. In the rule of Saint Columbanus, it simply says if one of the monks murders someone, he must be sent to another monastery. Now those were the robust ages. Always wish I had lived there.

So, no euphemism. And the other thing that everyone does, and you should not do, is recite categories. How ridiculous! This typical penitent actually makes up sins. Like Father, I was pusillanimous. I was querulous. I was guilty of callipygian cupidity and a slavering gulosity[50]. How can you be sorry for that? And how's the poor priest supposed to know what

---

[50] Excessive appetite, greediness. (<u>www.merriam-web-</u><u>ster.com</u>)

you're talking about? And how can he give an appropriate penance?

Another important thing: the priest has got to give an appropriate penance. If someone comes in and confesses to having an affair with his neighbor, what good does it do to give up ice cream for a week or say three Hail Marys? He could say those three Hail Marys with his neighbor, just divide it up. So it should be pertinent, as pertinent as doctors are when they give a particular medicine for a particular physical malady. A priest should give a particular penance that pertains to a particular spiritual malady.

And so, no euphemisms, and no categories, just a little story, a wee story about yourself and how you offend. How you subvert your exquisite humanity and the glory of Christ in you. Try to say what you think is the fundamental disorientation, if you like. What is the big omission in your life? Perhaps your biggest sin is an omission. Maybe you haven't read a book in a week. That's a pretty big sin, especially if you haven't read a Christ book, you haven't read the New Testament, in a week. I met a priest once who went six months without reading a spiritual book. Can you believe that? It's true. So omissions—not praying, not reading, not loving, not being responsible for the people, for the trees and the dogs of your parish. Think of all the sick in your town you don't even know about. 'Fess up. Ease up on administration, deepen ministry, pray Mass, play music.

One night I heard all these confessions. About fifty of them in a row. They made up sins. So many seemed so vapid. One lad came in and said, "Father, I was mooning on Broadway." Well, that's not a sin; it's an asinine recreation. I couldn't absolve him from that. I need a sin to absolve. So that's not a sin. Tell me something: how did you offend God? *That* delighted God. And since we live in such a dull, drab, dreary age, people should be driving down Broadway mooning more often. They're not. I may as well stay in my hermitage.

Another lad came in, and he confessed, "Father," he said, "I was Irish kissing in the church parking lot." Well, that's not a sin; it's a lost art, actually. You know, it's much better than French kissing. But no one knows how to do it anymore. A few old Celts do.

So then after hearing all this drivel, a middle-aged man came in; he was married and had a family. And he says, "Father, I don't have a list of anything but I want to tell you that my family's a mess, and I feel responsible. I think the problem is that I'm not a Christ man. I don't know Christ. I don't love Christ. And it seems there's no joy in the family. Christ is absent. The result is chaos. I'm sorry."

On hearing this I jumped up out of the confessional, ran around to where he knelt, and hugged him.

He was astonished, of course, and looked a bit stunned until I explained that out of fifty-some confessions I'd heard that evening his was the only one that was real. This man opened his heart to Christ and lamented the one thing really worth being sorry for: not being a Christ man, not being centered on Christ and his great love. In confessing his lack he had found the God of Mercy and been found by him. We must all go on doing that until love explodes in our hearts, in our lives, in all those near us. *That* is the way to go to confession.

A proper disposition for absolution is not always easy to achieve. Often a mindful exchange between priest and penitent is required. Until a tough member of the Mafia could say with tears flowing down his face, "I rode my horse to death," he was not ready to be forgiven. We need to be sorry and shame can be our last hope.

I don't know how anyone can bear the terrible, unbearable burden of sin for more than a few seconds. It's so terrible I don't know how people do that. And no one needs to do it because as soon as a person is sorry that he offended God and thus disturbed the whole universe, (because there's no such thing as a separate God) they open themselves to forgiveness. Yes, when I sin, since I am not an isolated human being, I break down the health of the whole mystical body of Christ, and I disturb the whole universe. The Cosmos, the galaxies, everything.

The effect of all that is loneliness, which is undoubtedly man's most awful experience. To be utterly lonely and to feel that you cannot *be*; that is a separate human being, an isolated human being. We feel it. Having sinned, we feel it. I know I personally feel it. I lived constantly and have lived for years on the edge of despair because I have sinned. But I know that that despair, if I am faithful to my God who is sheer love, will draw me into joy. If I penetrate the darkness, the emptiness, the ugly despair, the unbelievable fact that I have indeed offended my love, my beloved, the ultimate one—if I penetrate that, I will find on the other end, sheer mercy and joy.

We meditate on the crucifixion and we see the agony, we see the rejection, we see the blood, we hear the howling of the God-man: my God, my God where are you? There is the God-man, missing God his Father. And dying in love, alone. His Father is there, but as man he cannot feel him. He cannot sense him. My God, my God, why hast thou abandoned me? God seemingly abandoned him on the human mode. Not the divine mode. And that's what our sin did to Jesus the Christ. And that's what sin does to us in a negative way. When we sin, we are not on the verge of resurrection. We are not redeeming the human race by the agony that Christ suffered, as we indeed are when we suffer with Christ, for then we are co-redeemers with Christ.

When we sin, we disturb the whole creative process and the whole redemptive process, and we retard the human evolutionary process for maybe one thousand years or maybe ten times that. One sin can do that. And think of the millions and billions of sins being committed by millions and billions of people. And so the retardation of the human race. And so the ugliness, the atrocities, the mendacity of politicians and presidents and even sometimes ecclesiastical apparatchiks. So it permeates; the terrible lie of sin disorganizes our whole human condition.

And there's not much we can do about it. There's nothing we can do about it. But Christ has already done something about it. And that doing goes on. What Christ did was initiate all the marvels of God's love and mercy. He initiated all the wonders and all the miracles that characterize real Christianity. What we have got to do is to appropriate them, assimilate them, digest them, and make those gifts of God in Christ realizable. And we can't do that unless we're sorry that we sinned, unless we feel it at the core of our being.

I would prefer to say, however, that the basic philosophical problem is sin, how you cope with sin. Or better yet, how do you cope with otherness, with the Wholly Other, with God himself?

In the Gospel we find two ways of coping. Jesus presents this with such pellucid clarity in a graphic sort of way. There is the way Judas coped with his sin, and that was suicide. And there was the way that Peter coped, and that was by being a humble, flexible follower of Christ. He knew how to fall and get right up again relying, not on his own acquisitions or accomplishments, but upon the mercy of God. He could have gone on forever and ever, falling forever and ever, and it wouldn't matter that much because there was the mercy of God. Yes, coping with sin is indeed our greatest challenge. Oh! Maybe not. How about our coping with God! With the Cosmic Theandric[51] Presence?

How do we do it? Sin, strictly speaking, is the only evil in the world. And the problem with that is sin's inevitable kind of growth. We know that from what man has done to man. We know that from original sin. We know that from tracing the history of humankind back to Adam and Eve, tracing it right to our present day and the condition of today, which is, despite all kinds of technological and scientific progress, not better, but perhaps far worse. Saint Augustine lay it all out in three keyword: "*peccatum poena peccati*"[52]. That's one of my favorite quotes from any saint. In three words he just sums up the pain and the anguish, the fact that, as Alexander Pope said, man is "The glory, jest and

---

[51] Theandric: relating to, or existing by, the union of divine and human operation in Christ, or the joint agency of the divine and human nature.

[52] "The punishment of sin is sin."

riddle of the world." But *sin* is what knocks the stuffing out of us.

Peccatum poena peccati means this: the punishment of sin is sin. That's it. It's sort of redundant. And because of that we get trapped in it. It's terrifying, contagious. It's horrible. We get so immersed and stuck in sin, especially if it becomes a kind of respectable sin, the *pretty poison* we don't even notice. And so we live sinfully. We, in a respectable sort of way, defy God and pit ourselves against him, rather than living drenched in his mercy; falling but never, never meaning to sin and never settling for any kind of sin or the vestiges of sin. That's what Saint Augustine is referring to, *peccatum poena peccati*. There's a vestige of sin. And then one sin leads to another sin. And then we slip into a gentle, lawless lethargy.

The fact is we do that because we can't pull ourselves up by our own bootstraps. It's impossible. We can't save ourselves. We can't redeem ourselves. We can't just brush the sin away. We need a redeemer. We need a savior. We need the holy one, the ineffable one who loves us, loves to come and to touch us at deep levels of our being and to scorch us so that he cauterizes the sin. He is the doctor. He is the medicine man. He is the God-man. And he alone can save us from our sins.

So it's no problem, no ultimate problem, to fall or to sin. The ultimate problem would be to cope with it on our own steam. Or to ignore it, repress it. Not to face it, not to be humbled by it, and then not to confess it and be repentant and renewed and refreshed.